SETSWANA - ENGLISH
PHRASEBOOK

PUISANYO YA SEKGOWA
LE   SETSWANA

With a vocabulary and
short introduction to
grammar
by
A. J. WOOKEY

28 th Impression 2000

Revised Edition

ISBN 999 12 612 7 3

Printed by:
Printing and Publishing Company Botswana

A WARNING FROM THE EDITOR

This phrasebook is an attempt to bridge the communication gap and necessitate cross cultural interaction through the use of language. However, it can do more harm than good if it is used without sensitivity to avoid the retrograde attitude.

In the nature of such a book, many of the sayings here are brief, and would be curt if used just as they stand. Generally, in Setswana, the element of courtesy is expressed by starting or finishing them with 'rra' or 'mma'. For instance, 'O batlang?' just like that has the force of 'You - what do you want?', a rather peremptory enquiry implying that the person is a nuisance or that his presence there is suspicious. However, spoken gently as 'O batlang, rra?', the discourteous overtone disappears. Furthermore, where the occasion calls for greater politeness and courtesy, a better and more appropriate phrase is used ,such as, "A nka go thusa, rra?" (Can I help you, sir?).

As much as a Motswana can be offended by the insensitive use of his language, so too can an Englishman read the wrong feeling into what a Motswana says or does. For example, an Englishman might think a Motswana churlish if he accepted something without saying 'Thank you', while in fact he was expressing gratitude by taking the gift with two hands. On the other hand a Motswana would think an Englishman impolite if he were to snatch a gift with one hand, however vigorously he said 'Thank you'. A Motswana would feel offended if asked for direction by a stranger without being greeted first. But an English would view the same as a waste of valuable time.

This should be enough to convey the point that care is needed here if awkwardness and misunderstandings are to be avoided. The advice on page 7 about practising intonation with a member of the other race applies also in connection to attitudes and courtesies.

Steady M. Nkoane

TLHAGISO YA MORULAGANYI

Bukana e e kwadilwe ka maikaêlêlô a gore batho ba kgône go buisanya ka go kgabaganya molelwane wa diteme. Le fa go ntse jalo, e ka dira matshwênyêgô a magolo go feta tshiamô fa e dirisiwa ka go tlhoka go akanyetsa maikutlo a ba bangwegongwe ka go tlhoka go tlhaloganya go re go na le phatlha nngwe ya ngwaô fa gare.

Rona ba re leng Batswana re itse sentle go re mokgwa wa go supa maitseo ke go simolola puo kgotsa go e digela ka mafoko a a reng 'rra' kgotsa 'mma'. Ka Sekgowa ke tlwaêlô go dirisa lentswe la 'please' (ke go re 'tswêêtswêê) go nôlôfatsa ditaêlô kgotsa ditôpô. Jaaka fa re batla go re 'Bua ka bonya, rra' sentle ka Sekgowa ga re nke re re, 'Speak slowly' fela re bo re khutla foo, re tla a tshwanêla go re, 'Speak slowly, please'. E seng jalo gongwe re ka kgopisa yo re buang nae.

Ka ntlha e nngwe, le rona re se ka ra kgopisêga fa motlha mongwe Lekgowa le bonala e kete ga le na maitseo a a siameng ka fa mokgweng wa rona. Jaaka gongwe le ka re dumedisa fela la re 'Dumela' mme le sa digela ka 'rra' kgotsa 'mma'. Re gakologêlweng go re Sekgowa se dumedisa ka go re 'Good morning' fela kgotsa ka 'Hello' mme go bo go sena molato. Se re ka se lemogang fela ke go re ga a ise a ithute mekgwa ya rona.

Go kalo fela go supa gore re êlê tlhôkô thata tirisô ya dipuo tse di mo bukaneng e gore re tile matshwenyego a a ka re tlelang mo go buisanyeng ga rona. Kgakololô e e mo tsebeng ya 7 ka ga go tlhwaêla Lekgowa tsebe kafa le bitsang modumô wa mafoko ka teng go ntse fela jalo le ka ga dipharologano tsa mekgwa le maitseo a a supang tlotlo.

Mae S. Johnson

iv

PRONUNCIATION

a	*as in* 'father'	e.g. kala, a branch
b	*as in* 'bell'	baba, enemies
d	*as in* 'den'	disa, herd
e	*as the vowel in* 'rate'	bela, boil
ê	*as the vowel* in 'then'	êma, stand
f	*(fh) lighter than in English**	fêla, only, just
g	*as in Afrikaans,* or ch in 'loch'	gôga, pull
h	*as in* 'hat'	hula, graze
i	*as ee in* 'deep'	dilô, things
k, l, m, n,	*as in English*	
o	*as in* 'open'	rona, we, us
ô	*as ou* in 'ought'	bônê, they, them
p, r, s, t,	*as in English***	
u	*as oo in* 'boon'	ruta,teach
w	*as in* 'way'	wa, fall
y	*as in* 'yet'	tsamaya, go away
ng	*as in* 'sing-a-carol'	ngaka, doctor
ny	*as in* 'senior'	nyatsa, despise
kg	*is k with guttural g (above)*	kgomo ox
kh	*is k with aspirate (with breath)*	khumô, wealth
ph	*is p with aspirate (not f as in English)*	phala, an impala
th	*is t with aspirate (not as in* 'them')	thata, strength
tl	*as in* 'butler'	tla, come
tlh	*is tl with aspirate*	tlhaba, pierce
ts	*as in* 'mats'	tsela, way, path
tsh	*is ts with aspirate*	tshaba, flee
š	*as in* 'sheet'***	maši, milk
tšh	*as in* 'church'	tšhaba, tribe
tš	*is similar to* tšh *but without aspiration*	ntša, dog

(1) *The f or fh sound needs care; it is not the 'labio-dental' sound of English which is made between upper teeth and lower lip; it is the 'bilabial' sound, made between lips only, without the teeth.

(2) **Actually these 'unaspirated' (unbreathed) consonants are a little difficult, for English speech rarely aspirates these consonants, puts 'breath' with them; so a Motswana's ear hears us say, not 'two powerful kings,' but 'thoo phowerful khings'. It takes practice to pronounce the consonants without any breath at all.

(3) ***Roughly speaking, the southern tribes of the Batswana use š much more than do the northern ones, which use s in its place. In the south, the pronunciation is lešome (ten), šuba (hide), šwa (die), etc.: in the north it is lesome, suba, swa. But when this consonant is followed by vowels a, e, or i, it is sh in both south and north; ša (burn), šêba (look round), maši (milk).

(4) When two consonants occur together, each must be sounded; the first is 'syllabic'(i.e., a syllable by itself). E.g., nna is pronounced 'n-na',mma is 'm-ma', rra is 'r-ra'; etc.

(5) There are no diphthongs; if two or more vowels occur together, each must be fully sounded, e.g., kua, shout, sia, outrun, boa, turn back.

1. As a general rule, in reading or speaking Setswana, the accent or emphasis falls on the last syllable but one in a word or sentence; as

Mo**dum**ô,	a noise;
Du**mê**la,	Good day;
Ke a mo **ra**ta,	I love him.
Ba letse ba tsamaile **tha**ta	They went a long way yesterday.
Ka**ê**la motho yo **tse**la	Show this person the road.

2. But when the last word ends in ng, the accent is on the last syllable, *e.g.,*

Dumê**lang**; Modi**mong**; mo **rateng.**

Metsi a a bela jaa**nong**	The water is boiling now.
Basadi ga ba yô mo gae;	The women are not at home;
ba ile didi**beng**	they have gone to the wells.

3. Should the sentence or phrase end in a word of one syllable, the accent is on the preceding vowel, *e.g.,*

Go swa	to die.
Wa me	of me.
A o bona noka, **ke** e?	Do you see this river?
Batho ba le bantsi ba **tla** tla	Many people will come.
Ke ôna motse **wa** bô, le wa gaetsho	This is their town, and mine too.

4. An adverb or preposition of one syllable, however, at the end of a sentence, partly takes the accent, as

Dula **fa,**	Sit here.
Dikgomo tsa bônê **di** mo	Their oxen are in here.
Pitse ke a e bona, **e kwa**	I see a horse, it is there (a good bit off).

5   If rra or rrê, my father, or mma or mmê, my mother, is the last word in a sentence the accent falls on the last syllable, e.g.,

Ditsala tsa ga **rrê**	My father's friends.
Ntlo ya ga m**mê**	My mother's house.

6   Syllables always end with a vowel except when they end in **ng**, or sometimes colloquially **m** or **n**.

SETSWANA and ENGLISH
PHRASES

The English and Setswana languages are fundamentally different in their methods of expression, and so there are many pitfalls into which a learner of the other language can fall. For instance, the "tone" and "intonation" of the phrase is governed according to different rules in each language. In Setswana, what are apparently the same words can express two meanings according to the "tune" to which they are said. *Ke motho* can mean either I *am a person* or *It is a person*. It is therefore strongly recommended that the learner of Setswana should rehearse the phrases with a Motswana before using them.

E re ka,puo ya Setswana e fapaana thata le ya Sekgowa mo go bitseng mafoko, e ka re gongwe morutwana wa Sekgowa a timediwa ke go bitsa medumô ya mafoko a Sekgowa jaaka a bidiwa mo Setswaneng, gongwe ke go tlhaela go lemoga pharologanyo nngwe e e tshwanetseng go nna teng. Go tsaya sekai, *cough* le *dough* ke mafoko a medumô ya ônê e lebegang e tshwana fela, mme totatota e farologanye thata. Moithuti wa Sekgowa o tshwanetse go tlhwaêla pitso ya mafoko a Sekgowa tsebe jaaka a bidiwa ke Makgowa ka osi, le go ithutuntsha go a bitsa jalo.

Ditumediso	**Greetings**
Dumela, dumelang *(sing and pl)*	Good morning, or good afternoon. *(sing. and pl.)*
Dumela morena	Good morning, sir!
Dumela mohumagadi!	Good morning, madam!
Sala sentlê	Goodbye, or remain nicely; *spoken by the one going away to the one remaining.*
Tsamaya sentle	Goodbye, or go away nicely; *spoken by the one remaining to the one going away.*
Rôbala sentlê	Good night, or sleep nicely.
O tswa kae?	Where do you come from? *(sing.).*

Lo tswa kae?	Where do you come from? (Pl.)
O ya kae?	Where are you going to?
O mang?	Who are you? (sing.)
Lo bomang?	Who are you? (pl.)
A o sa tsogile sentle?	Are you quite well?
Ee, ke sa tsogile	Yes, I am quite well.
Nnyaa, ga ke a tsoga sentle	No, I am not well.
Dikgang ke eng?	What's the news?
Ga go na dikgang	There is no news.

Tshimologô ya puo	**Introductory**
Nako ke mang?	What is the time?
O batlang?	What do you want? (sing.)
Lo batlang?	What do you want? (pl.)
Wêna o senka mang?	You, whom do you seek?
O a reng?	What do you say?
O agile kae?	Where do you live?
Ke agile kwa Taung	I live at Taung.
Ke agile mono Vryburg	I live here in Vryburg.
Ntlo e ke ya ga mang?	Whose house is this?
Ke ntlo ya me	It is my house.
Ke ntlo ya ga rrê	It is my father's house.
Motse o ke ofe?	What town is this?
Ke Molepolole	It is Molepolole.
Tsêna	Come in or Go in.
Dula fa, *kgotsa,* Nna fa	Sit here.
Setilo ke se	Here is a chair.
Motho yole ke mang?	Who is that person?
Ga ke itse	I don't know.
Nna/dula fa fatshe	Sit on the ground or Sit down.
Nna/dula fale	Sit over there.
Nna/dula kwa	Sit yonder.
O ntse sentlê	He is all right.
Êma fa	Stand here or Come here (being polite).
O eme kwa	He is standing there.
Bua sentlê	Speak nicely.
Bua ka bonya	Speak slowly.
Ga ke utlwe	I do not hear.
Ke a utlwa	I hear.
Ba utlwile	They have heard.

Ga ke bone	I do not see.
O jelê nala / O etile.	She has gone out visiting.
Ke a bôna	I see.
Ke bonye	I have seen.
Ba tla a bôna	They will see.
A o letse o robetse?	Did you sleep last night?
A lo tsogile sentlê?	Are you well this morning?
Ee, re tsogile	Yes, we are well.
A o itse Setswana?	Do you know Setswana?
A o bua Setswana?	Do you speak Setswana?
Nnyaa, ga ke se itse	No, I do not know it.
Ke se itse go le gonnye	I know it a little.
Ee, Nnyaa	Yes, No
A o na le ditsala?	Have you any friends?
Ee, di teng/gônê	Yes, there are, or, I have.
Nnyaa, ga di yô	No, there are none.
Di kwa kae?	Where are they?
Ba dirile sentlê	They (people) have done well.
Motho a le mongwe fêla	One person only.
Basadi ba le babedi	Two women.
Banna ba le bararo	Three men.

Mafoko a Lolwapa

Household Phrases

Gaetsho ke fa	This is where I live.
Monna wa me	My husband (man).
Mosadi wa me	My wife (woman).
Ke ngwanakê	It is my child.
Ke bana ba me	They are my children.
Bitsa mosimane yole	Call yonder boy / Call that boy.
Ya le mosetsana yo	Go with this girl.
Ngwana o tsogile	The child is up, or, awake.
Ngwana o a lela	The child is crying.
Tsosa bana/banyana	Waken the children.
Ba siêlê maši	Give them some milk
Apesa ngwana/ngwanyana	Dress the child.
Tlhapisa bana/banyana	Wash the children.
A o itse go bolêla lobaka ka tloloko?	Can you tell the time by the clock?
Ke lobaka lwa go tsoga	It is time to get up.
Mo rwese tlhoro / hutshe	Put her hat on for her.

Mo rwese ditlhako	Put on his shoes for him.
Lere ditlhako tsa me	Bring my shoes.
Rwala hutshe le ditlhako	Put on (your) hat and shoes.
Rola hutshe	Take off your hat.
Rola ditlhako	Take off your shoes.
Baakanya bolaô	Make the bed.
Robatsa ngwana/ngwanyana	Put the child to sleep.
Tshêla metsi mo mogopong	Put water into the bowl.
Gotlha ditlhako	Clean the boots.
Lere sephimolô/taolê/toulô	Bring the towel.
Lere molôra	Bring the soap.
Go bothithô thata gompieno	It is very warm to-day.
A ngwanyana a isiwê kwa ntlê	Let the child be taken out of doors.
A se ke a nna mo letsatsing	Let him not be in the sun.
Rôbala, rôbalang	Go to sleep (sing. and pl.).
Gotsa molelô	Light the fire.
Tshuba lobônê	Light the lamp.
Lere dikgong	Bring some wood.
Fêêla ntlo	Sweep the house.
Phimola dilwana	Wipe the utensils.
Udubatsa diphatê	Shake the rugs, or carpets.
Bula ntlo	Open the house (door).
Tswala ntlo	Shut / Close the house (door).
Bula fenestere	Open the window.
Tlhatlaya ketlele	Put on the kettle.
Metsi a a bela	The water boils (is boiling).
Tlhatswa dilô tse	Wash these things.
Ya sedibeng	Go to the well.
Sediba se kae?	Where is the well?
Ya go ga mo sedibeng	Go to the well for water.
Leina la gago ke mang?	What is your name?
Leina la gagwê ke mang?	What is his name?
Leina la me ke Johane	My name is John.
A o bua Sekgowa?	Do you speak English?
Nnyaa, ke bua Seburu	No, I speak Afrikaans.
Re tsile, ba tsile	We have come, they have come.
O tla a tla leng?	When will he come?
Kgetse e, ke ya ga mang?	Whose bag is this?
Sejana se thubilwe ke mang?	Who broke this dish?

Se ne se le metsi — It was wet.
Se reletse mo diatleng tsa me — It slipped out of my hands.
Fensetere e, e leswê — This window is dirty.
A e phimolwê thata ka letsela — Let it be well wiped with a rag.
Tlhapa matlhô — Wash your face.
Tlhapa tlhogo — Wash your head.
Tlhapa dinao — Wash your feet.
Kwala leina la gago — Write your name.

Go Apaya — Cooking

A go rathwê dikgong — Split up some wood.
O se ka wa tlhadia metsi thata — Don't put too much water.
A dikgong di sa le dintsi? — Is there still plenty of wood?
Lere tse dingwe — Bring some more (wood).
Tsholola metsi — Throw away the water.
Tshêla mo pitseng — Pour into the pot.
Tlhatlaya pitsa — Put on the pot.
Apaya dijô — Cook the food (with water).
Apaya jaanong jaana — Cook at once.
Re tla a ja ka sethôbôlôkô — We will eat at twelve o'clock.
Obola makwele/ditapolê — Peel the patatoes.
Besa nama — Roast the meat.
Nama e budule — The meat is cooked.
Tlhatswa digwêtê — Wash the carrots.
Segêlêla dikwii/anyanse — Cut up the onions.
Tsenya mo pitseng — Put into the pot.
A o itse go duba borôthô — Can you knead bread?
Baakanya sebedisô — Make the yeast ready.
Duba sentlê — Knead well.
Lere boupe gapê — Bring more flour.
A bo belê — Let it rise.
Bo bedile — It has risen.
Tsenya mo isong — Put into the oven.
Tshola ka sejana se — Take up on this dish.
Apaya nama ya kgomo — Cook the beef.
Sejana se phanyegile — The dish is cracked.
Se thubegile — It is broken.
Sega nama — Cut the meat.
Thipa e kae? — Where is the knife?
Thipa ke e — Here is the knife.
Bogôbê ga bo a butswa — The porridge is not done.

Tlhatswa pitsa	Wash the pot.
Loka ka letswai	Put in salt.
Go a ša	It is burning.
O dirang?	What are you doing?
O raya mang?	Whom do you mean?
Ke raya mosimane yo	I mean this boy.
Dira thata	Work hard.
Siana thata	Run fast.
Ke raya wêna	I mean you.
Akofa, akofang	Make haste *(sing. and pl.)*.
Dira ka bonakô	Make haste (at work).
Tsamaya ka bonakô	Go quickly.
Lere molôra	Bring the soap.
Tlhapa diatla	Wash your hands.

Mo Loetong — On a Journey

A kara e golêgwê	Let the cart be inspanned.
Golêga koloi	Inspan the wagon.
A e tshasiwe	Let (the wheels) be greased.
Ke batla metsi	I want water.
Ke batla dijô	I want food.
Ke bolailwe ke tlala	I am hungry.
Ke bolailwe ke letsatsi/lenyôra	I am thirsty.
A o jelê?	Have you eaten?
Ga ke ise ke je	I have not eaten yet.
A o nolê?	Have you drunk?
Ga ke ise ke nwe	I have not drunk yet.
Dijô ke tse	Here is some food.
Metsi ke a	Here is some water.
Mpolêlêla	Tell me.
Mmolêlêlê	Tell him (or her).
Ke dijô tse di monate	It is nice food.
A o a mpôna?	Do you see me?
A o a mmôna?	Do you see him?
Ee, ke a go bôna	Yes, I see you.
A o kile wa mpôna?	Have you seen me before?
Gokêlêla pitse mo sesaneng	Tie up the horse to the post.
Golêga dipitse	Inspan the horses.
Golêga dikgorno	Inspan the oxen.
A re tsamayeng	Let us go.
Golola	Make loose, or, outspan.

Ya nokeng	Go to the river.
Gêlêlêla swaki	Fill the water cask.
Baya dilwana mo koloing.	Put the things in the wagon.
Gokêlêla dilwana thata gore di se latlhêgê	Tie the things fast so that they don't get lost.
Ya go rêka borôthô	Go to buy some bread.
Faga tee, kana kofi	Make the tea or coffee.
Tshêla maši mo teng	Pour milk into the tea.
Tsenya/loka sukere	Put sugar in.
Hudua ka loswana	Stir with a spoon.
Lere dithipa	Bring the knives.
Le dintshwana le dikomoki	And the spoons and cups.
Sega borôthô	Cut the bread.
Phutha dilwana	Collect the things.
Dilwana di mo letloleng	The things are in the box.
Go lekanye	It is enough.
Ga go a lekana	It is not enough.
Le galê	Just so.
Ga ke na sepê	I don't care.
A o a nkutlwa?	Do you hear (understand) me?
Nkgogisa/Nkgoisa	Give me some tobacco.
Ke lapile	I am tired.
A go kgakala kwa motseng?	Is it far to town?
A mogobe o sa le kgakala?	Is the pan still far off?
Tshwara pitse	Catch the horse.
Pitse e kete e batla metsi	The horse looks as if it wants water.
Isa pitse kwa metsing	Take the horse to the water.
Belesa pitse gore ke pagamê	Saddle the horse that I may ride
E solê, e mohuhutsô thata	Rub it down, it has a good deal of sweat.
Fa dipitse furu/fabore	Give the horses forage.
Nngwe le nngwe ya ngata.	Each one bundle.
Thupa ya me e olê	My sjambok has fallen.
A ko o e nnêêlê	Please give it to me.
Seme se latlhegile	The whip is lost.
Dikgomo tseo ga di goge	Those oxen do not pull.
Di betsê!	Whip them up!
Tsela e thata	The road is heavy.
A tsela e na le majê?	Is the road stony?
A go sa le kgakala kwa metsing?	Is it still far to the water?

13

Golola dikgomo di hulê	Outspan the oxen, to graze.
Nosa dipholo	Water the oxen.
Di tla a gokêlêlwa mo dijokweng bosigo	They must be tied to the yokes at night.
Naga e, e na le ditau	There are lions in this veld.
Dikgomo di timetse	The oxen have wandered / gone astray.
Di sa le di tsamaya bosigo	They went away in the night.
Fa o rata, o ka tsamaya	If you wish, you can go.
Kgwanyakgwanya fa setswalong	Knock at the door.
Tsela e kae?	Where is the road?
Tsela ke e	Here is the road.
Ga go na tsela	There is no road.
Pitse e a tlhotsa	The horse is lame.
Fa nkabo ke itsile nkabo ke se ka ka e palama	If I had known I would not have ridden it.
Maoto a koloi a repile	The wheels are loose.
A a isiwe mothuding	Take them to the smith.
A a kgaolwê	Let them be shortened.
Letsatsi le tlhabile	The sun has risen.
Letsatsi le phirimile	The sun has set.
Go sa le motshegare	It is still daytime.
Go bosigo	It is night.
Go ngwedi	It is moonlight.
Go lehihi (lefifi)	It is dark.
A o tle o tseye dilô tse e seng tsa gago?	Do you take things which are not your own?
Nnyaa, ga ke utswe	No, I do not steal.
Madi ke a, ya go rêka ditêmpê	Here is money, go and buy some stamps.
Ya kwa tlung ya pôsô	Go to the post office.
E kwa kae?	Where is it?
Botsa batho mo motseng	Enquire of the people in the town.
Ntlo ya thutô/kêrêkê e kae?	Where is the church?
Ya kwa go Mmakaseterata	Go to the Magistrate.
Ke romilwe kwa go ênê	I am sent on a message to him.
A o kile wa ya gônê?	Have you been there before?
Nnyaa, ga ke ise ke ye	No, I have not yet been.
Segêlêla motsoko	Cut up the tobacco.
O se ka wa bua jalo	Do not speak like that.

A o itse go bala?	Can you read?
A o itse go kwala?	Can you write?
A o Mokeresete?	Are you a Christian?
Ee, ke wa phuthêgô	Yes, I am a church member.
Nnyaa, ke motho fêla	No, I am an ordinary person.
A ga go na dikwalo?	Are there no letters (or books)?
Ya go botsa dikwalô kwa posong	Go and ask if there are letters at the post.
Ya go pôsa dikwalô	Go post the letters.
Isa lokwalô lo kwa go Rrê-	Take this letter to Mr.-
Tshwara thata fa	Hold fast here.
Tsholetsa matlole	Lift up the boxes.
A bêyê mo majeng	Put them on stones.
Bitsa mosimane yo monnye	Call the little boy.
Lokwalô lo kae?	Where is the letter / book?
A o ko o mphê dijô	Please give me some food.
Ntshupetsa ditshwantshô	Show me the pictures.
Tshasa dikgôlê mahura	Grease the harness or riems.
O tshêgang?	What are you laughing at?
Ke ênê yo o re bolaisang ditshêgô	It is he who makes us laugh.
A kgosi e mo gae?	Is the chief at home?
Nnyaa, e pagame e ile morakeng	No, he has ridden to the cattle-post.
Dumedisa kgosi	Greet the chief.
Ke kopa dijô le diaparô	I beg food and clothes.
Mpha madi	Give me money.
Ga re a tshola madi	We have no money with us.
Gama kgomo	Milk the cow.
A e na le maši?	Has it any milk?
Ga e na maši	It has no milk.
Lere madila ke a rêkê	Bring some sour milk that I may buy it.
Ke batla maši a lobese	I want some fresh milk.
Gama dipodi	Milk the goats.
O tla a tlhaba nku ka mosô	You will slaughter the sheep in the morning.
Dikgomo di kae?	Where are the cattle?
Di mo sakeng	They are in the kraal.
Di kwa nageng	They are in the veld.
O direlang jalo?	Why does he do so?
Dira jaana	Do thus.

15

Tla ka mosô	Come tomorrow.
Ba letse ba gorogile	They arrived yesterday.
Ke tla a tlhôla mono	I shall stay the day here.
Ke tla a lala mono	I shall sleep (spend night) here.
A pula e a na?	Is it raining?
Ee, e na thata	Yes, it is raining hard.
Phakêla thata	Get up very early in morning.
Go la bokae?/Go letsatsi mang?	What day is it?
Go Tshipi (la Morena)	It is Sunday.
Ke lwa boraro	It is the third day (Wednesday).
Ke kgwedi mang?	What month is it?
Ke ngwaga wa bokaye?	What year is it?
Kana o bonya jang!	How slow you are!
Naga e ntlê thata	The veld is very good.
Bojang bo bontsi/gônê thata	There is plenty of grass.

Tshimo — Field/Garden

A re yeng tshingwaneng	Let us go to the field.
Nosa tshingwana	Water the garden.
A ditlhare di nosiwê	Let the trees be watered.
Le tsônê ditšheše/dithunya	And the flowers.
A se na le loungô?	Has it any fruit?
Loungô lo sentswê ke seramê	The fruit has been destroyed by the cold.
Dilô tse di swabile	These things are dried up.
Dinônyane di ja dipeo	Birds eat the seeds.
Ee, ke magakabe	Yes, it is the crows.
Kumola mofero o	Pull up these weeds.
Epa sebata se	Dig this patch.
Epa mahuti fa, re tlhomê ditlhatshana tse	Dig holes here, to plant these plants in.
Tlhagola makwele/ditapolê	Weed the potatoes.
Dipeo di tlaa jalwa fa	Seeds will be sown here.
Lere mogala	Bring the line.
Nosa tshingwana yotlhe	Water the whole garden.
Tlhagola ditsela	Weed the paths.
Lere garawe le haraka	Bring the spade and rake.
A o na le tiro?/mmêrêkô	Have you any work
Nnyaa, ga ke na tiro/mmêrêkô	No, I have no work.
Ke tla a tla ka mosô	I will come in the morning.
Kala e, a e kgaolwê	Let this branch be cut off.

A ba lemile mabêlê a Setswana?	Have they planted Setswana corn?
Nnyaa, ke korong	No, it is wheat.
O tla a bôna Pula/Ranta ka letsatsi	You shall have twenty cents a day.
A ke tla a bôna dijô?	Shall I have some food?
Ee, o tla a di bona,	Yes, you shall have some, if
fa o dira sentlê	you work well.
Ke duêla ka madi	I pay in cash.
Gangwe fêla ka beke	Once a week.
Ke tle ke duele ka Matlhatsô	I usually pay on Saturday.

Go Tlhatswa — Washing

A re tlhatswê dikhai/diaparô	Let us wash the clothes.
Re di tlhatswê kae?	Where shall we wash them?
A kwa nokeng kgotsa mo gae?	At the river or at home?
Lo se ka lwa tlhatswetsa mo forong	Don't wash clothes in the furrow.
Tlhatswetsa kwa ntlê	Wash outside
Lere metsi a mantlê	Bring clean water.
Se lere metsi a a leswê	Don't bring dirty water.
Tshasa molôra o di sugê thata	Smear with soap and rub them well.
Molôra o, o molemô mme o a tura	This soap is good, but it is expensive.
O se ka wa o senya fêla.	Do not waste it.
Tsenya dikhai/diaparô mometsing pele	Put the clothes into water first
A dikhai/diaparô di anêgwê	Let the clothes be put out to dry.
A di ômile?	Are they dry?
Ga di ise di ôme	They are not dry yet.
Di ômile, a di phuthwê	They are dry, let them be collected.
A re gatise dilwana	Let us iron the clothes.
Di kgatshê pele, o di menê	Sprinkle and fold them
Besa dikgatiso	Put the irons to the fire.
Tshuba kgatisô	Put on the iron(electric)
A dikhai di gatisiwê	Let the clothes be mangled.

Go Roka — Sewing

A re rokeng	Let us sew.
Lere letsela	Bring the cloth.

Setswana	English
Sega letsela jaana	Cut the cloth thus.
Sômêla lomaô	Thread the needle.
Lere sekêrê	Bring the scissors.
Roka sentle ka botswerere	Sew nicely with skill.
Kgaola tlhale	Cut off the cotton.
Gokêla talama (konopo) fa	Sew a button on here.
Ditalama ga di a lekana	There are not enough buttons.
Ya go senka tse dingwe kwa bentleleng	Go to get some more at the shop.
Phunya letshoba (leroba) fa	Make a hole here.
A le rokwê, ke la talama	Let it be sewn, it is for a button.
A o itse go roka ka matšhine	Can you sew with a machine?
Bitia ka sebata se	Put on this patch.
Dibolola sebata se	Cut out this patch.
Dira ka fa sekaong se	Work by this pattern.

Letsomô — Hunting

Setswana	English
A re yeng go tsoma	Let us go to hunt.
Tsaya tlhôbôlô	Take the gun.
Tshola panta le marumô	Carry the belt and cartridges.
A dithôlô di gônê?	Are there any kudus?
Ga di yô	There are none.
Dikgaka di mo sekgweng se	Guinea fowl are in this thicket
Nônyane ke e	Here is a bird.
Phuduhudu ke ele	There is a steenbuck.
Photi e robetse fa	A duiker is asleep here.
Tshêphê e ka bonwa kae?	Where can a springbok be found?
Bitsa ntša	Call the dog.
A ntša e, e ka tshwara mmutla?	Can this dog catch a hare?
Masogo a mo bojannyeng	Partridges are in the grass.
Mmutla o mo tlhageng e	A hare is in this cover.
Dihudi di mo kgophung (mokgatšheng)	Wild ducks are on the valley.
Ya go sêla nônyane	Go and pick up the bird.
Kgori e tsamaya fale	A pauw is walking yonder.
A e bolailwe?	Is it killed?
E tlhabilwe (gobetse) fêla	It is only wounded.
Ke e fositse	I have missed it.
Go bosigo, a re boêlê kwa gae	It is night (late), let us return home.

Ngaka	Doctor
A re yeng ngakeng	Let us go to the doctor.
A ngaka e mo gae?	Is the doctor at home?
Ee, e mo gae	Yes, he is at home.
A o a lwala?	Are you ill?
Ee, ke a lwala	Yes, I am ill.
O lwala fa kae?	Where are you ill?
Seatla sa me se botlhôko	My hand is in pain.
Nthô e, e botlhoko	This sore is painful.
A mmele wa gago o molelô?	Are you hot?
Nnyaa, ke sitilwe thata	No, I am very cold.
Ke ôpiwa ke tlhôgô	My head aches.
Lere letsôgô (lebôgô)	Give me your hand (arm).
A mala a gago a botlhoko?	Is your stomach in pain?
Marapô a me a a phaphanya.	My bones ache.
A o tlo o ye kgorong?	Do you ever go to the loo?
A mokôtla o botlhoko?	Have you a pain in your back?
Ee, le mo marapong otlhe	Yes, and in all my bones.
Ke bolawa ke letshoroma	I have malarial fewer.
Ke itshegile ka thipa	I cut myself with a knife.
Mma ke e fapê ka letsela	Let me bandage it.
Nwa molemô o	Drink this medicine.
Rôbala fa	Lie down here.
Ke bolawa ke setlhabi	I have a pain in my chest.
Mohama o, o botlhoko	This side is painful.
Go botlhoko makgwafo	The lungs are sore.
Itsukulê ka molemô	Gargle with this medicine.
O kgwê	Spit it out.
Dikgopo tsa me di botlhoko	My ribs are sore.
A o tle o tlhatse?/o kgwe?	Do you vomit?
Mometso o rurugile	The throat is swollen.
Ke tshwerwe ke sedidi	I am giddy.
A lerapô le robegile?	Is the bone broken?
Ga ke itse	I don't know.
A mafatlha (sehuba) a botlhoko?	Is your chest sore?
A o a gôtlhôla?	Do you cough?
Leitlhô le botlhoko	(My) eye is sore.
A selô se mo teng?/A o fatlhilwe?	Is anything in it?
Mmele wa me o rokomologile	There is a rash on my body.
Mma ke bônê	Let me see.
Lebêla kwa tlase	Look down.

Lebêla kwa godimo	Look up.
A tsêbê e botlhoko?	Is the ear painful?
Nnyaa, go botlhoko leinô	No, it's the tooth that is painful.
A ke tlhagala kgotsa boswa?	Is it an abcess or a tumour?
Go botlhoko maoto le dinao	The legs and feet are painful.
Didimala, o se ka wa lela	Be quiet, do not cry
Monwana wa me o botlhoko	My finger (or toe) is sore.
Dinao tsotlhe di botlhoko	Both feet are painful.
A o tlhapologa sentlê?	Do you pass water easily?
A o moimana?	Is she expecting a baby?
O simolotsê leng go lwala?	When did you begin to be ill?
Ke bogologolo (kgalê)	It is a long time ago.
A ga o ise o nne botoka?	Are you no better yet?
Ke botokanyana (kaone)	I am a little better.
Ke fodile sentlê	I am quite well.
Ke a leboga, ke a itumêla	I thank you, I am glad.
Tuêlô e tla a nna bokae?	How much will it cost?

Mafoko Fêla   General Expressions

Ngwana wa ga kgaitsadiakê o sule/o tlhôkafetse	My sister's child is dead.
O tla a fitlhwa gompieno	He will be buried today.
A ko o tlê phitlhông	Do come to the funeral.
A ko o mphê ntšhe	Please give me some sweet reed.
Borrago le mmago ba kae?	Where are your father and mother?
Borrê le mmê ba ile masimo	My father and mother have gone to the fields (lands).
A a bitsê rraagwê le mmaagwê	Let him call his father and mother.
Dumêla mma; dumêla rra	Good morning, madam (mother) good morning, sir (father).
Leina la gago ke mang?	What is your name?
Kana/Ana go tsididi jang!	How cold it is!
Go bothithô thata	It is very warm.
Go molelô (mogote)	It is hot.
O bolêla mafoko a mantlê	He tells good news.
Ke eng? Ga se sepê	What is it? It is nothing.
O rwele nkgwana	She is carrying a water pot.
O e isa kwa motseng	She is taking it to the town.

Gaeno ke kae?	Where is your home (abode)?
Gaetsho ke kwa Têêmaneng	My place is at Kimberley.
O ile kwa ga gabô	He has gone to his place.
Tsoga ka bonakô	Get up quickly.
Apara, aparang	Dress yourself, or yourselves.
Apola diaparô	Undress yourself.
Tlosa malele/mabebe a	Take away this rubbish.
A latlhêlê kgakala	Throw it far away.
Lere metsi a a bothithô	Bring (some) warm water.
Lere metsi a a tsedidi (maruru)	Bring (some) cold water
Leba kwano o nnêêlê selêpê	Look this way and hand me the axe.
Tirô ya gago ke eng	What is your work?
O dingwaga di kae?	How old is he?
A motho yo botlhale	What a wise person!
Ga a botlhale	He is not wise.
A motho wa mogolo!	Poor soul!

Kwa Borekelong (Mmaraka) — At the Market

Tsaya tlatlana (seroto) re tsamaê	Take the basket and let us go
Dikgong tse di a rekisiwa	This wood is for sale.
Mae a ke bokae?	How much are the eggs?
O tla a ntsha bokae?	How much money will you give?
Ke tla a tlisa mmidi ka kgwedi e e tlang	I will bring mealies next month.
Go makwele/ditapolê le merôgô	There are potatoes and greens.
Ke batla maungô	I want fruit.
A go rekwê nama	Let some meat be bought.
Mma ke tsênê	Let me come in.
A koloi e fetê	Let the wagon pass.
Motho yoo o tla go tsietsa	That man will cheat you.
Ke tla a tla gapê mo bentleleng eno	I will come again to this shop.
A ko o nnêêlê tšhentšhe ya me	Please give me my change.
Tsenya mo sekaleng	Put it on the scales.
Tšhêkê e, ke ya Pula tse tlhano	This cheque is for P5.
Thêbê/Disêntê tse tlhano	Five Thebe/Cents
Kwala leina la gago ka fa moragô ga yônê	Write your name on the back of it.
Ba tla a go nêêla madi ka yônê	They will give you cash for it

kwa bankeng	at the bank.
Gongwe o tla a bona madi ka yônê kwa bentleleng	Or you may get cash for it at the shop.
Mo go mong wa yônê bentlele	From the shopkeeper.
Kobô e, e lôpa bokae?	How much is this kaross?
Selô se, ke bokae?	How much is this thing?
Se tshwanetse go ja (bôna, lôpa) go feta foo.	It ought to get more than that.
Go siame/lekanye, ke a dumêla	It is enough, I agree.
Ke itumetse	I am satisfied (happy).
Ke a itumêla	Thank you.
A o na le madi?	Have you any money?
Nyaa, ga ke na naô	No, I have none.
Ke na le a le mannye	I have a little
O rêkang?	What are you buying?
Ga ke reke sepê	I am not buying anything.
A re yê koo, a re yeng koo	Let us go *(dual and pl)*
Tsenya madi a gago mo bankeng ya Pôsô	Put your money in the Post Office bank.

Koloi ya Molelô/ Terena

Train

Terena e tla a gôrôga leng?	When will the train arrive?
Seteišene se kae?	Where is the station?
Rêka thekethe	Buy a ticket.
A o tshotsê pasa?	Have you a passport?
Thekethe e lôpa bokaye?	How much is the ticket?
Tshola mofagô le metsi	Take some food and water.
A kara e tlê go ntsaya	Let the cart come for me.
Le fa e le pitse	Or a horse.
A go na le hôtêlê?	Is there an hotel?
A go ka rôbalwa gônê?	Can we sleep there?
Ee, malaô a mantlê	Yes, the beds are nice.

Go êma (Nyalô)

To be married

Ba êma(nyalana) gompieno	They are to be married today.
Moruti o tla a ba emisa (nyadisa)	The minister will marry them.
Go modirô wa kêmô (lenyalô)	There is a wedding feast.
O na le mosadi/O nyetse	He has a wife.
O na le monna/O nyetswe	She has a husband.
Ga a na mosadi/Ga a nyala	He has no wife.
O motlhôlagadi	She is a widow.

O dingwaga di kae?	How old are you?
A ke gônê o nyalang (êmang)?	Is this the first time you marry?
A o itse go kwala?	Can you write?
A batsadi ba gago ba dumalana?	Do your parents agree?

Kwa Posong / At the Post Office

Isa lokwalô lo kwa ofising ya megala	Take this letter to the telegraph-office.
O bo o letê phetolô	And wait for an answer.
Madi a a duêlang ke a	Here is the money to pay with.
Go tswetswe	It is closed.
Nnyaa, ga go ise go tswalwe	No, it is not closed yet.
Go tle go bulwe ka 9	It opens at 9 o'clock.
Go tle go tswalwe ka 5	It closes at five.

Dilô tsa legae / Things of home

A go na le dikoko?	Are there any fowls (chickens)?
Dingwenyana di gônê/teng	There are a few.
A di nonnê?	Are they fat?
Di a bopama/Di mekôgô	They are thin.
A di fiwê mabêlê	Let them have some corn.
Di tshêlêlê metsi	Give them water.
Ga go na mae	There are no eggs.
Ga di ise di bee (tsale)	They have not begun to lay.
Tse dingwe di a elama	Some are sitting.
Tse dingwe di na le dikokwana	Others have chickens.
Di bolawa ke bobeleise	They have vermin.
Go na le phagê e e di bolayang	There is a wild cat which kills them.
A ga se nakedi?	Is it not a polecat?
Segootsane se tle se di phamole	The hawk takes them off.
Rêka dikoko tse dinamagadi	Buy some hens.
A mokoko o o nonneng o bolawê	Let the cock which is fat be killed.
Maši a podi a monate	Goat's milk is good (tasty).
A go rêkwê dipodi tse di namagadi	Let some ewe goats be bought.
Katse o bolaile pêba	The cat has killed a mouse.
Dipêba di senya dikgetse	The mice are destroying the sacks.
A di thaisiwê ka serai (selaga)	Let the trap be set for them.

23

Ntša e bogola eng?	What is the dog barking at?
E bogola motho	It is barking at a person.
A e a loma?	Does it bite?
Nnyaa, ga e lome	No, it does not bite.
E bogola fêla	It only barks.
Ntša ya me e tlhatsitse	My dog has pups.
Ke tla a go naya nngwe di sena go gola	I will give you one when they have grown.
Kolobê e tswaletswe	The pig is shut up.
A hôkô ya yônê e nnê phepa	Let its sty be clean.
A e fiwê dijô tse di phepa	Let it have clean food.
Foo nama ya yônê e tla a nna monate.	Then its flesh will be nice (tasty).
A e ja merôgô?	Does it eat green stuff?
Ee, le masetô a makwele, le a maphutshe	Yes, and the peelings of potatoes and pumpkins.
Ke eng?	What is it?
Se kae?	Where is it?
Leina la selô se ke eng?	What is the name of this thing?
Ntsosa maphakela (ka bosigo)	Get me up early.
O ise o fage kofi	Before you make coffee.

INTRODUCTION TO GRAMMAR

NOUNS - MAINA

A NOUN is the name of any thing or person, or place; *as,* dog, John, Cape Town.

NOUN, ke leina la selô sengwe le sengwe, le fa e le la motho, kgotsa la felô; *jaaka* ntša, Johane, Kapa.

Singular/Bongwe
Ke selô se le sengwe *jaaka*
Axe, selêpê
Ox, pholo
Box, letlole

Plural/Bontsi
Ke bobedi kgotsa bontsi jwa dilô; *jaaka*
Axes, dilêpê.
Oxen, dipholo.
Boxes, matlole.

In English the *plural is* generally shown by adding the suffix 's' to the word, *as* Boy, boys; axe, axes.

Ka Sekgowa *bontsi* bo supiwa ka go oketsa lefoko ka tlhaka ya 's', *jaaka* Boy, boys; axe, axes.

In Setswana the plural is indicated by prefixing letters, or by changing the first syllable; *as*

Ka Setswana *bontsi* bo supiwa ka go baya ditlhaka ka fa tshimologong ya lefoko le fa e le ka go fetola ditlhaka tsa tlha; *jaaka*

Thipa, **di**thipa;
tomati, **di**mati.

Thipa, **di**thipa;
selêpê, **di**lêpê.

NOUNS in Setswana are of various classes, each class being distinguished by its prefix; the prefixes also denote the number; whether the Noun is singular or plural. In Nos. 8 and 9 the prefix is wanting in the singular. The classes are numbered for convenient reference.

Noun Class	Singular	Plural	Examples
1	mo	ba	motho, person; batho, persons (people).
2	mo	me	motse, town; metse, towns.

3	mo	ma	moôka, mimosa; meôka, mimosas
4	se	di	sediba, a well (borehole); didiba, wells (boreholes).
5	lo	di	lonaka, a horn; dinaka, horns.
6	bo	ma	bosigo, night; masigo, nights.
7	le	ma	lentswê, a stone (rock); majê, stones (rocks).
8	-	di	kgosi, a chief; dikgosi, chiefs.
9	-	bo	ntšhe, ostrich; bontšhe, ostriches.
10	go	ma	go lema, ploughing; malemô, ploughings.

Class I is characterised by personal nouns.

Class 3 is chiefly composed of names of trees.

Class 9 is a small class, mainly names of a few animals, and is used for many foreign names of things.

Class 10 is the infinitive used as a noun.

A large number of trees of the same kind is indicated by changing the prefix 'mo' to 'lo'; *e.g.,*

Loôka, a thicket of mimosa.

Very many animals of the same kind are indicated by the prefix ma; *e.g.,*

Magomo, very many cattle; from kgomo, a cow (ox).

Mabodi very many goats; from podi, a goat.

PRONOUNS - MAEMEDI

A PRONOUN is a word which stands in place of a Noun. (Leina),

MAEMEDI ke lefoko le le êmang mo boemong jwa Noun ke go re, Leemedi.

Singular/Bongwe

OF PERSONS

I; ke, nna
You; o, wêna
He; o, ênê
She; o, ênê
It is I; ke nna
It is you; ke wêna
It is he; ke ênê
It is she; ke ênê

OF THINGS

It; o, se, lo, bo, le, e, go
Kgomo e a tsamaya;
the ox is going away.
Setlhare se eme;
the tree is standing.
Lo fano; it is here.

Plural/Bontsi

JWA BATHO

We; re, rona.
You; lo, lona, nyêna.
They; ba, bônê, bôna.
They; ba, bônê, bôna.
It is we; ke rona.
It is you; ke lona.
It is they; ke bônê.

JWA DILÔ FELA

They; e, di, a, ba.
They are running;
di a taboga.
They are looking; ba lebile.
They will come; di tla a tla.
They are there; di kwa.

Possessive

In English the Possessive is
shown by, **of**, *as* the horns **of**
the ox; or by adding **'s** to the
end of the word, *as,* the boy**'s**
father; or if it already ends in s,
by adding **'** only, *as* Moses**'**
father.

In Setswana the Possessive
is shown by the use of the
Particles with the Noun, or
with the Possessive Pronoun.
The Nouns with various prefixes have each their own
particles, in singular and plural,
as Seatla sa me, my hand
Dikobô tsa mosadi, the woman's
karosses/blankets

Lerui

Ka Sekgowa Lerui le supiwa
ka, 'of', *jaaka* (the horns **of**
the ox) dinaka **tsa** kgomo; le ka
go kwala "**s**" ka fa bofelong
jwa lefoko, *jaaka* (the **boy's**
father) rragwe mosimane; me
e re fa go setse go na le '**s**'
gônê go kwalwe jaana:
(Mos**es'** father) rraagwê Moše.

Ka Setswana, Lerui le
supiwa ka mafokonyana a a
pataganang le Leina (Noun), le
fa e le Leemedi. Leina lengwe
le lengwe le na le lefokonyana
le le rulaganang nalô *jaaka*

Seatla sa me; my hand
Dikobô tsa mosadi; the
woman's karosses/blankets

27

Before the name of a person 'ga' is used, *as*

Dikgomo tsa **ga** Kgama, Kgama's oxen

Fa e le leina la motho go bewa 'ga' fa pele ga lônê, *jaaka*
Dikgomo tsa **ga** Kgama. Kgama's oxen.

POSSESSIVE PRONOUNS
PERSONAL

1-me; my, mine
  gago; your, yours
  gagwê; his, her, hers,

MAEMEDI A MARUI
A BATHO

rona; our, ours.
lona; your, yours.
bôna or bônê; their, theirs.

OF THINGS

A DILO FELA

Singular/Bongwe			*Plural/Bontsi*		
2—ôna	its,	it	2—yôna	theirs,	they
3—ôna	its,	it	3—ôna	theirs,	they
4—sôna	its,	it	4—tsôna	theirs,	they
5—lôna	its,	it	5—tsôna	theirs,	they
6—lôna	its,	it	6—ôna	theirs,	they
7—lôna	its,	it	7—ôna	theirs,	they
8—yôna	its,	it	8—tsôna	theirs,	they
9—gagwê	its,	it	9—bôna	theirs,	they
10—gôna	its,	it	10—ôna	theirs,	they

PARTICLES WITH POSSESSIVE

Singular			*Plural*		
1- **mo**, prefix, takes **wa**			1- **ba**, prefix takes **ba**		
2- mo	"	**wa**	2-me	"	**ya**
3- mo	"	**wa**	3-ma	"	**a**
4- se	"	**sa**	4-di	"	**tsa**
5- lo	"	**lwa**	5-di	"	**tsa**
6- bo	"	**jwa**	6-ma	"	**a**
7- le	"	**ja** *or* **la**	7-ma	"	**a**
8-	"	**ya**	8-di	"	**tsa**
9-	"	**ba**	9-bo	"	**ba**
I 0-go	"	**ga**	10-ma	"	**a**

DIKAÔ	EXAMPLES
Mosadi wa me	My wife.
Basadi ba rona	Our wives.
Motse wa me	My town.
Metse ya me	My towns.
Mokala wa me	My camel thorn.
Makala a me	My camel thorns.
Selêpê sa gago	Your axe.
Dilêpê tsa me	My axes.
Sekhurumêlô sa yôna	Its lid.
Lobônê lwa me	My candle.
Dipônê tsa me	My candles.
Ditlhakô tsa yonê	Its hooves.
Bogosi jwa me.	My kingdom.
Magosi a gagwê	His kingdoms.
Letlole la me	My box.
Matlole a rona	Our boxes.
Mênô a tsôna	Their teeth.
Thipa ya me	My knife.
Dithipa tsa lona	Your knives.
Kala ya ôna	Its branch.
Loungô lwa sôna	Its fruit.
Kgôrô ya yônê	Its entrance.
Ntšhe wa me	My ostrich.
Bontšhe ba bônê	Their ostriches.
Go êpa ga tsôna	Their digging.
Maêpô a tsônê	Their diggings.
Dikwalô tsa banyana	The children's books.
Dipodi tsa ga rrê	My father's goats.
Moroki wa mosese	The sewer of the dress.
Bareki ba mabêlê	Buyers of corn.
Lolwapa lwa mosadi wa gagwê	His wife's court-yard.
Kgetse ya mosetsana yo	This girl's bag.
Mafoko a kgosi	The chief's words.
Botswerere jwa modiri	The workman's skill.
Letsôgô la ngwanyana	The child's arm.
Molodi wa nônyane	The bird's singing.
Megoma ya Sekgowa	English ploughs.
Mofine wa Kapa	A Cape vine.
Mmusô wa kgosi	The King's government.

Palamente ya Makgowa	English Parliament.
Ditlhako tsa pitse	The horse's hoofs.
Megatla ya dinku	The tails of the sheep.
Mênô a ntša	The dog's teeth.
Mênô a dintša	The dogs' teeth.

VERBS - MADIRI

A verb is a word which expresses being, or doing, or being done; *as*	Lediri ke lefoko le le kayang go nna, kgotsa go dira le fa e le go dirwa; *jaaka*
I see	Ke a bôna.
The ox is drinking	Kgomo e a nwa.
He is sitting	O ntse (dutse).
She is being called	O a bidiwa.

TENSE	LOBAKA
Present tense	Ke lobaka lwa jaana.
Future tense	Ke mo go tla a tlang (nnang).
Past tense	Ke mo go fetileng.
Perfect tense	Ke mo go setseng go fetile.
Imperfect tense	Ke mo go ne go dirwa.
Negative	Ke mo go sa dirweng, mme go supiwa ka, **ga, le sa, le se**.
	Ka Sekgowa, go supiwa ka **not**.

Go rêka	**To buy**

LOBABA LWA JAANA	PRESENT TENSE
Ke a rêka	I am buying.
O a rêka	You are buying
O a rêka	He is buying.
Re a rêka	We are buying.
Lo a rêka	You are buying.
Ba a rêka	They are buying.
Ga ke reke	I am not buying.
Ga o reke	You are not buying.
Ga a reke	He is not buying.
Ga re reke	We are not buying.
Ga lo reke	You are not buying.
Ga ba reke	They are not buying.

PAKA E E TLANG

	FUTURE
Ke tla a rêka	I shall buy.
O tla a rêka	You will buy.
O tla a rêka	He will buy.
Re tla a rêka	We will buy.
Lo tla a rêka	You will buy.
Ba tla a rêka	They will buy.
Ga ke **nka** ke rêka	I shall not buy.
Ga o **nka** o rêka	You will not buy.
Ga a **nka** a rêka	He will not buy.
Ga re **nka** re rêka	We will not buy.
Ga lo **nka** lo rêka	You will not buy.
Ga ba **nka** ba rêka	They will not buy.

Instead of **nka** in FUTURE NEGATIVE, some say **ketla**, or **na**; e.g., Ga a **ketla** a rêka, He will not buy.

Ga a **na** a rêka.

MO GO SETSENG GO FEDILE

	PERFECT
Ke rekile	I have bought.
O rekile	You have bought.
O rekile	He has bought.
Re rekile	We have bought.
Lo rekile	You have bought.
Ba rekile	They have bought.
Ga ke a rêka	I have not bought.
Ga o a rêka	You have not bought.
Ga a a rêka	He has not bought.
Ga re a rêka	We have not bought.
Ga lo a rêka	You have not bought.
Ga ba a rêka	They have not bought.

MO GO NE GO DIRWA

	IMPERFECT
Ke ne ke rêka	I was buying.
O ne o rêka	You are buying.
O ne a rêka	He was buying.
Re ne re rêka	We were buying.
Lo ne lo rêka	You were buying.
Ba ne ba rêka	They were buying.

31

Ke ne ke sa reke	I was not buying.
O ne o sa reke	You were not buying.
O ne a sa reke	He was not buying.
Re ne re sa reke	We were not buying.
Lo ne lo sa reke	You were not buying.
Ba ne ba sa reke	They were not buying.

NEGETIVE INCOMPLETE	**KGANETSO YA TIRO E E SA FELELANG**
Ga ke ise ke reke	I have not yet bought.
Ga o ise o reke	You have not yet bought.
Ga a ise a reke	He has not yet bought.
Ga re ise re reke	We have not yet bought.
Ga lo ise lo reke	You have not yet bought.
Ga ba ise ba reke	They have not yet bought.

NOTE:- The *Perfect* of the Verb is usually formed by changing final **a** to **ile**; but the ending :

êla	becomes	**etse**	bolêla	tell	*pf.*	boletse
ala	"	etse	bônala	visible	"	bonetse
ola	"	otsê	golola	loose	"	golotsê
ara	"	ere	tshwara	seize	"	tshwere
sa	"	sitse	disa	herd	"	disitse
tsa	"	ditse	botsa	ask	"	boditse
na	"	nye	bôna	see	"	bonye
na	"	nne	rona	misfit	"	ronne
ma	"	me	palama	climb	"	palame
nya	"	ntsê	fenya	conquer	"	fentsê
ôla	"	odile	bola	rot	"	bodile

NOTE:-The Pronoun must always come between the Noun and Verb; e.g.,

| Mosimane **o** rêka thipa | The boy buys a knife. |
| Motho yole **o** bonye kgomo | That person has seen the ox. |

When a Noun, etc., follows the Verb in the *present* tense the final **a** of the Pronoun is dropped; e.g.,

Ke (a) rêka pitsa	I am buying a pot.
O itse go dira sentlê	He knows how to work well.
Re tsamaêla ruri.jaanong	We are going away for good now

32

The Personal Pronouns *nominative are:*

Ke, I   Re, we,
O, you (thou)   Lo, you.
O and **a** he, she   Ba, they.

The other Pronouns for Nouns with or without *prefixes* with the
Verb are:

PRESENT TENSE

Bongwe		*Singular*
o	it,	Motse o a ša	The town/village is burning.
o	it,	Mofatlha o a omêlêla	The vaal bush is drying up.
se	it,	Selêpê se a rêma	The axe cuts.
lo	it,	Lobônê lo a tuka	The lamp is burning.
bo	it,	Bothata bo a gola	The difficulty is increasing.
le	it,	Letlole le a senyêga	The box is perishing.
e	it,	Kgomo e a fula	The ox is grazing.
o	it,	Ntšhe o a siana	The ostrich is running.
go	it,	Go lema go a tswêlêla	The ploughing is going on.

The *Plural* of these are:

e	they,	Metse e a ša	The towns are burning.
a	they,	Mafatlha a a omêlêla	The vaal bushes are drying up.
di	they,	Dilêpê di a rêma	The axes cut.
di	they,	Dipônê di a tuka	The lamps are burning.
a	they,	Mathata a a gola	The difficulties increase.
a	they,	Matlole a a senyêga	The boxes are perishing.
di	they,	Dikgomo di a fula	The oxen are grazing.
ba	they,	Bontšhe ba a taboga	The ostriches are running.
a	they,	Malemô a a tswêlêla	The ploughing are going on.

For Negative Present, put **ga** before the Pronoun, which drops
final **a**, and final **a** of Verb becomes **e**; *e.g.,*

Motse ga o še,   The town is not burning.
Dikgomo ga di hule,   The oxen are not grazing.

Imperative

Bongwe	*Singular*
A ke rêkê	Let me buy.
A ke se rêkê *or* / A ke se ka ka rêka	Let me not buy.
Rêka, or, a ko o rêkê	Buy.
Se rêkê, or, o se ka wa rêka	Do not buy.
A a rêkê	Let him buy.
A a se rêkê	Let him not buy.
	Dual
A re rêkê	Let us buy.
A re se rêkê	Let us not buy.
Bontsi	***Plural***
A re rekeng	Let us buy.
A re se reke	Let us not buy.
Rêkang, or / Lo rêkê, or, lo rêkeng	Buy.
Se rêkeng, or, / Lo se ka lwa rêka	Do not buy.
A ba rêkê	Let them buy.
A ba se rêkê	Let them not buy.

Pronous with the **Verb**, for various classes of nouns except the 1st are:

	Imperfect Singular
2-Motse o no o o ša	The town was burning.
3-Mofatlha o no o omêlêla	The vaal bush was drying up.
4-Selêpê se ne se rêma	The axe was cutting.
5-Lobônê lo ne lo tuka	The lamp was burning.
6-Bothata bo ne bo gota	The difficulty was increasing.
7-Letlole le ne le senyêga	The box was perishing.
8-Kgomo e ne e fula	The ox was grazing. .
9-Ntšhe o ne a taboga	The ostrich was running.
10-Go lema go ne go tswêlêla	The ploughing was going on.

	Imperfect Plural
2-Metse e ne e e ša	The towns were burning.
3-Mafatlha a ne a ômêlêla	The vaal bushes were drying up.

4-Dilêpê di ne di rêma	The axes were cutting.
5-Dipônê di ne di tuka	The candles were burning.
6-Mathata a ne a gola	The difficulties were increasing.
7-Matlole a ne a senyêga	The boxes were perishing.
8-Dikgomo di ne di fula	The oxen were grazing.
9-Bontšhe ba ne ba taboga	The ostriches were running.
10-Malemô a ne a tswêlêla	The ploughings were going on.

For *Negative Imperfect,* put **sa** before the Verb, and change final **a** to **e**; *e.g.,*
Selêpê se ne se **sa** reme, The axe was not cutting.

Future Singular

2-Motse o tla a ša	The town will burn.
3-Mofatlha o tla a ômêlêla	The vaal bush will dry up.
4-Selêpê se tla a rêma	The axe will cut.
5-Lobônê lo tla a tuka	The candle will burn.
6-Bothata bo tla a gola	The difficulty will increase.
7-Letlole le tla a senyêga	The box will perish.
8-Kgomo e tla a fula	The ox will graze.
9-Ntšhe o tla a taboga	The ostrich will run.
10-Go lema go tla a tswêlêla	The ploughing will go on.

Future Plural

2-Metse e tla a ša	The towns will burn.
3-Mafatlha a tla a ômêlêla	The vaal bushes will dry up.
4-Dilêpê di tla a rêma	The axes will cut.
5-Dipônê di tla a tuka	The lamps will burn.
6-Mathata a tla a gola	The difficulties will increase.
7-Matlole a tla a senyêga	The boxes will perish.
8-Dikgomo di tla a fula	The oxen will graze.
9-Bontšhe ba tla a siana	The ostriches will run.
10-Malemô a tla a tswêlêla	The ploughing will go on.

For *Negative Future,* put **ga** before the Pronoun, and change as follows:

Motse **ga** o na o o ša	The town will not burn.
Dilêpê **ga** di na di rêma	The axes will not chop.

35

Kgotsa

Motse ga o ketla/nka o o ša
Dilêpê ga di ketla/nka di rêma

Or

The town will not burn.
The axes will not chop.

Nakô e e tlang -Past Tense
Go gana, To refuse; pf., ganne.

BONGWE

SINGULAR

Tumalano
Ke ne ka gana
O ne wa gana
O ne a gana
Re ne ra gana
Lo ne lwa gana
Ba ne ba gana

Affirmative
I refused, or, I did refuse.
You refused, **or,** you did refuse.
He refused, or, he did refuse.
We refused, or, we did refuse.
You refused, or, you did refuse.
They refused, or, they did
  refuse.

Kganetso
Ga ke a ka ka gana
Ga o a ka wa gana
Ga a ka a gana
Ga re a ka ra gana
Ga lo a ka lwa gana
Ga ba a ka ba gana
Ga e a ka ya gana

Negative
I did not refuse.
You did not refuse.
She did not refuse.
We did not refuse.
You did not refuse.
They did not refuse.
It did not refuse.

2, 3, O ne wa gana
  4, Se ne sa gana
  5, Lo ne lwa gana
  6, Bo ne jwa gana
  7, Le ne la gana
  8, E ne ya gana
  9, O ne a gana
 10, Go ne ga gana

Ga o a ka wa gana.
Ga se a ka sa gana.
Ga lo a ka lwa gana.
Ga bo a ka jwa gana.
Ga le a ka la gana.
Ga e a ka ya gana
Ga a ka a gana.
Ga go a ka ga gana.

PLURAL
They refused.
2, E ne ya gana
3, 6, 7, 10, A ne a gana
4, 5, 8, Di ne tsa gana

BONTSI
They did not refuse.
Ga e a ka ya gana.
Ga a ka a gana.
Ga di a ka tsa gana.

36

9, Ba ne ba gana   Ga ba a ka ba gana.
Ga lo a tshwanêla go nwa bojalwa   You ought not to drink beer.
Bogolo rêkang dilô tse di thusang   Rather buy helpful things.
Bojalwa jwa Sekgowa bo a senya   White people's drink destroys.
After **gore**, that, or, so that, the   Verb generally ends in **ê**.
Mmitsê **gore** a utlwê   Call him that he may hear.

THE VERB "TO BE"

It is often expressed by the Pronoun; e.g.,

Ke moagi   I am a builder.
O botlhale   He/She/You are wise.
O mmetli   You are/He is a carpenter.
Ke mmetli   He/It is a carpenter.
Re baagi   We are builders.
Lo baagi   You are builders.
Ba/Ke babetli   They are carpenters.
Go, it is, before an Adjective.
Go ne go le   it was, before an Adjective.
Go tla a nna   it will be.
Ke, it is, they are, before a Noun or Pronoun.
E ne e le   it was, they were, before a Noun or Pronoun.
E tla a nna   it will be, before a Noun or Pronoun.

Go lefifi   It is dark.
Go go ntlê   It is well.
Go ne go le bosula   It was bad.
Go tla a nna metsi,   It will be wet.
Ke kgomo   It is an ox/cow.
Ke dikgomo   They are oxen/cows.

To be, Go nna, the pf. *ntse* is used as the present, e.g., Se ntse, it is.
Ke ntse jalo   I am so.
Di ntse sentlê   they are all right.

Le also expresses *to be*; e.g., o ne a le gônê/teng, he was there
E ne e le motho   It was a person.
E ne e le batho   It was, or, they were people.
Go, or, go na le   There is, or, there are.
Go ne go le   There was, or, there were.

Go tla a nna, There will be, before Nouns, Pronouns and
Adjectives.

Forms of the Verb

PASSIVE of the Verb is formed by putting **w** before the final vowel.

Pitsa e a rêkwa	The pot is being bought.
Nku e tlhabilwe	The sheep is slaughtered.
A pitse e belesiwê	Let the horse be saddled.

CAUSATIVE of most Verbs is formed by changing final **a** into
isa; which (in pf.) becomes **isitse**.
Go rata, To love.   Go rat**isa**, To cause to love.
Rat**isitse**, Have caused to love.
Go tsama**ya**, To go, Go tsama**isa**, To cause to go.

RELATIVE is formed by changing final **a** into **êla**.
Go rat**êla**, To love for, *(Pf.)*   ratetse, have loved fort
Ke tla a mo rek**êla** kobô   I will buy a kaross for him,

RECIPRPOCAL is formed by changing final **a** into **ana**.
Go rat**ana**. To love one another. (pf.)
Ba ratanye. They have loved one another.

VERBS ending in **êga** are intransitive, and have the force of the
verbal ending **-able** in English; e.g.,

o a rata,	he loves.
o a rat**êga**,	he is lovable.
go ruta,	to teach.
go rut**êga**	to be teachable.

Verbs ending in **fala** have the force of become; e.g.,

go dira	to do.
go dira**fala**	to become done, or, come to pass.

REVERSIVE is formed by changing final **a** to **olola**; *e.g.,* go dira,
to do; go dir**olola**, to undo; pf., dir**olotsê**.

REFLEXIVE is formed by prefixing **i** to a verb; e.g., dirêla, to work
for; go **i**tirêla, to work for oneself; Pf., **i**tiretse.

DEMONSTRATIVE PRONOUNS

Motho yo	This person.	Motho yole	That person.
Batho ba	these people.	Batho bale	Those people.
Nku e	This sheep.	Nku ele	That sheep.
Dinku tse	These sheep.	Dinku tsele	Those sheep.
Leru le	This cloud.	Leru lele	That cloud.
Maru a	These clouds.	Maru a le	Those clouds.
Bojang jo	This grass.	Bojang jo le	That grass.
Majang a	These grasses.	Majang a le	Those grasses.
Lorakô lo	This wall.	Lorakô lo le	That wall.
Marakô a	These walls.	Dithakô tse le	Those walls.
Setlhare se	This tree.	Setlhare sele	That tree.
Lomati lo	This plank.	Lomati lo le	That plank.
Motswi o	This arrow.	Metswi e le	Those arrows.
Go lema mo	This ploughing	Malemo a le	Those ploughings.

O added to the Demonstrative Pronoun instead of **le**, indicates **that** viz., something near the person spoken to-e.g., selêpê se**o**, that axe; thipa e**o**, that knife.

PERSONAL PRONOUNS

OBJECTIVE		EMPHATIC	
n, m	me.	nna	I, me.
go	you, thee.	wêna	you, thou, thee.
mo, m	him, or, her.	ênê	he, him.
re	us.	rona	we, us.
lo	you.	lona	you.
ba	them.	bônê	they, them.

OBJECTIVE Pronouns come before the Verb; **n** and **m**, of *first person singular* are prefixed to the Verb, *as*

Mpôna, see me, from **m** and **bôna**.
Nthuta, teach me, from **n** and **ruta** as **n** and **r** become **nth**.
M of the *third person* for **mo**, is also prefixed to the Verb when the first letter is **b**, when it changes the **b** also to **m**, *as*
Mmônê, see him, for **mo bônê**.

EMPHATIC Pronouns come after the Verb; *as*

Ke ênê	it is he.
E ne e le sônê	It was it.
E tla a bo e le bônê	It will be they.
Naya/Nêêla nna	give me.
Ke batla yônê	I want it, **or,** That is the one I want.
Ke nna	It is I.
Ke wêna	It is you.
Ke a go senka/batla	I am seeking you.
Ke raya wêna	I mean you.
Ke a go rata	I like you.
Ba a di bôna	they see them.
Re thusê	help us.
O a mo rata	she loves him.
O mmiditse	he has called her.

RELATIVE PRONOUNS

USED ALSO AS ADJECTIVES

Motho yo o bônang	The person who sees.
Batho ba ba bônang	The people who see.
Molapô o o tletseng	The full river.
Melapô e e tletseng	Full rivers.
Nokana e nnye	A small stream.
Metsi a mantlê	Clean water.
Mokala o o tlhogang	A sprouting camel-thorns.
Makala a a tlhogang	Sprouting camel-thorns.
Lomati lo lo thata	A strong board.
Dimati tse di thata	Strong boards.
Dikgong tse ditelele	Long pieces of wood.
Pitse e e ragang	A kicking horse.
Dipitse tse di ragang	Kicking horses.
Lentswê/Lejê le le godileng	A high mountain.
Majê a a godileng	High mountains.
Bogosi jo bo bokoa	A weak kingdom.
Magosi a a bokoa	Weak kingdoms.
Go lema mo go maswê	Bad ploughing.
Ntšhe yo motona (tonna)	A big ostrich.
Bontšhe ba batona (tonna)	Big ostriches.

After the Relative Pronoun the Verb ends in **ng**.

ALL (THE WHOLE)

	Singular				Plural		
1	**mo**	makes	yotlhe	fêla	1	**ba**	makes	botlhe	fêla
2	**mo**	„	otlhe	„	2	**me**	„	yotlhe
3	**mo**	„	otlhe	„	3	**ma**	„	otlhe
4	**se**	„	sotlhe	„	4	**di**	„	tsotlhe
5	**lo**	„	lotlhe	„	5	**di**	„	tsotlhe
6	**bo**	„	jotlhe	„	6	**ma**	„	otlhe
7	**le**	„	jotlhe	„	7	**ma**	„	otlhe
8	**e**	„	yotlhe	„	8	**di**	„	tsotlhe
9	**o**	„	yotlhe	„	9	**bo**	„	botlhe
10	**go**	„	gotlhe	„	10	**ma**	„	otlhe

Dikgomo tsotlhe fêla All the oxen.
Molato otlhe fêla The whole debt.

THE DIMUNITIVE of the Noun is indicated by the termination **nyana**; Mosimane, a boy; mosima**nyana**, a little boy.

THE ADJECTIVE

An Adjective is a word which stands with a Noun to qualify it, or to show what kind of a person, or thing, it is e.g. a good

LETLHAODI

Letlhaodi (Adjective) ke lefoko le le êmang le Leina (noun), go le tlatsa, le go supa ka fa motho, le fa e le selô se boy, a long stick.ntseng ka gônê; jaaka mosimane yo molemô, thupa e telete.

Kgolo	great.	Nnye	little.
Ntlê	pretty.	Pôtlana	few.
Tshesane	narrow.	Tona (tonna)	large.
Ntsho	black.	Khutshwane	short.
Tshweu	white.	Telele	long.
Maswê	nasty.	Leswê	dirty.

A nice ox. Kgomo e ntlê.
A narrow path. Tsela e tshesane.
A little water. Metsi a mannye.

Nouns with their Relative Pronouns are also used as Adjectives as: Motho yo o molemô, a good person, or, a person who is good; motho, a person, molemô, goodness.

Tšhaka e e bogale, a sharp sword, or, a sword which is sharp.

Verbs in the perfect tense are also used as Adjectives; *as,* Noka e e atlhameng, a wide river; noka - a river, atlhame the perfect of atlhama - to be wide, with the Relative Pronoun **e e**, and Verb ending in **ng**, which always follows after the Relative Pronoun with the Verb; *as,*

Mokgwa o, e ne e le o o siameng, this custom was a right one. **Siameng** from **siama**, to be right, pf., **siame**.

ENGLISH —SETSWANA
VOCABULARY

In the word-list which follows, NOUNS are given in singular and plural where both forms exist. Thus:
Abscess, an, tlhagala (singular), ditlhagala (plural)
Night, bosigo (singular) masigo (plural).
In the case of VERBS, their present and perfect forms are given.
Thus:
Accept, to, tshola (present), tshotsê (perfect)
Try, to, leka (present) lekile (perfect).

Able	nonofile	Alter, to	fetola, fetotsê
Above	godimo ga	And	le
Abscess, an	tlhagala, ditlhagala	Angry	kgopilwe, gaketse
		Angry, he is	o gaketse, o tenegile
Accept, to	tshola, tshotsê	Answer, to	araba, arabile; fetola, fetotsê
Accuse, to	naya molato		
Accuse falsely, to,	pateletsa	Answer, an	karabô; phetolô
		Ant	tshoswane, ditshoswane
Accustomed, to be,	tlwaetse; lemetse	Antelope	phôlôgôlô, diphôlôgôlô
Add, to	oketsa, okeditse		
Advice	kgakololô	April	Moranang
Advise, to	gakolola gakolotsê	Arm	letsôgô, mabôgô
		Army	ntwa, dintwa
Adze, an	petlo, dipetlo	Arrive, to	fitlha, fitlhile; gôrôga, gôrôgile
After	moragô ga	Artery, an	losika lwa madi, ditshika tsa madi
Afternoon	maitsibowa tshokologo		
Afterwards	moragô	As, like	jaaka, fêla jaaka
Again	gapê	Ashes	molôra, melôra
Agree, to	dumalana, dumalanye	Ask for, to	1ôpa, lopile
		Ask, to enquire	botsa, boditse

Agreement	tumalanô	Asleep, he is	o robetse
Alike, to be	tshwana	Assemble, to	phuthêga
Alive, tshedile	utlwa	Assembly, an	phuthêgô, pitsô
All	tlhe, with the various prefixes, **bo**, **tso**, **yo**, **o**, etc.	Astray, to go	timêla, timetse
Also	le gônê	At	kwa, kwa go
August	Phatwê	Bend, to	ôba, obile
Avoid, to	tila, tidile	Bent, to be	obegile, kgopame
Awl, an	thokô, dithokô	Berry, a	kungwa, dikungwa
Axe, an	selêpê, dilêpê	Better	molemô, bogolo
		Better, to	befodile
		Better, is	botoka, kaone
Baboon	tshwene, ditshwene	Between	fa gare, fa gare ga
Baby	ngwana, bana lesea, masea	Beware, to	itisa, itisitse; tlhalefa
Backwards	kwa moragô	Bewitch, to	lôa, loile
Bad	maswê, bosula	Big	tonna, tona, kgolo, kgaraga with Relative Pronouns
Back	mokôtla, mekôtla	Bind, to	bôfa, bofile
Bag, a	kgetse, dikgetse	Bind up, to	fapa, fapile
Bake, to	besa, besitse	Bird	nônyane, dinônyane
Bark, to	bogola	Birth, to give	bêlêga, belege
Bark, of tree	lekwati, makwati	(of people)	tshola
Bask, in sun	sekamêla	Birth, to give	tsala, tsetse
Basin	sejêlô, dijêlô	(of animals)	
Basket, a	seroto, diroto	Birthday	letsatsi la botsalô
Be, to	nna, ntse	Bit, a	tomo, mogala
Beads	dibaga, ditalama	Bit (a piece)	kabetla
Bear, to	bêlêga, belege	Bite, to	loma, lomile
Beard	ditedu	Black	ntsho, with Relative Pronouns
Beat, to	betsa, beditse		
Because	ka, ka ntlha ya gore; ka gobo	Blanket	kobô, dikobô
		Bleed, to	tswa madi

44

Bed	bolaô, malaô	Bless, to	tshegofatsa, segofatsa
Beef	nama ya kgomo	Blessing, a	lesegô; tshegofatso; letlhôgônôlô
Beer	bojalwa	Blind person	sefofu, difofu
Beetle	khukhwane, dikhukhwane	Blind, to be	foufala, foufetse
Before	pele, fa pele ga	Blood	madi.
Beg, to	kopa, kopile	Bloom, to	thunya, thuntsê
Begin, to	simolola, simolotsê	Blow, to	budula
Beginning	tshimologô	Blow the fire	futswêla molelô
Behind	moragô ga	Blow, of wind	foka, fokile,
Belief	tumêlô	Blunt	boboi
Believe, to	dumêla, dumetse	Board	lomati, dimati
Bell, a	tshipi, tlôlôkô	Boast, to	belafala
Below	tlase ga	Boat	mokôrô, mekôrô
Bellows	mouba	Body	mmele, mebele
Belt	lebantê, mabantê	Body, dead	setoto, ditoto
Belt, to put on	ipantê	Boil, a	sesô, disô
Boil, to	bela, bedile	Bye and bye	kgantelê
Boil, to make to	bedisa		
Bone	lerapô, marapô		
Book	lokwalô, dikwalô	Calabash	segwana
Bore, to	phunya, phuntsê	Calf	namane, dinamane
Borrow, to	adima, adimile		
Boundary	molelwane	Calico	furumo
Bowels	mala	Call, a	pitsô, dipitsô
Bowl	mogotswana, megotswana	Call, to	bitsa, biditse
		Camp	bothibêlêlô
Box	letlole, matlole	Can	ka: o ka ya, he can go
Boy	mosimane, basimane	Carbuncle, a	kwatsi
		Carpenter	mmetli wa dikgong
Brains	bobôkô		
Branch	kala, dikala		
Break, to	kgaoga, kgaogile	Carrots	digwêtê

	(as a string)	Carry, to	tsaya or tshola
Break, to	rôba, robile	Pfs. tsere, tshotsê, also rwala, rwele	
Break, in pieces	thuba, thubile	Cartridge	sekôtlôpô
Breast	lebêlê, mabê1ê	Cat, pole cat	nakedi; wild cat,
Brick	setena, ditena		phage
Bright, to be	phatsima	Catch, to	tshwara, tshwere
Bring, to	lere, lerile	Caterpillar	seboko, diboko
Broken in pieces	thubegile, phatlakane	Cattle	matlhape
Broom	lefêêlô, diphêê1ô	Cave, a	logaga, dikgaga
Broth	morô	Chaff	mmoko
Build, to	aga, agile	Chain, a (a chain ornament)	kêêtane, teu, sekagêlê
Builder, a	moagi, baagi		
Building, a	kagô, dikagô	Chair, a	setilô, ditilô
Bull, a	pôô, dipôô	Change, to	fetola, fetotsê
Burn, to	ša, selê	Changed, to be	fetogile,
Burn, to	fisa, fisitse; (causative)	Charm, a	pheko, dipheko
		Charm, to	phekola, phekotsê
Burn, to, as fire, candle, etc.	tuka, tukile	Chase, to	lê1êka,lelekile; alola; koba
		Cheat, to	tsietsa, tsieditse
Bury, to	fitlha, fitlhile	Cheek, a	lerama, marama
Bush, a	setlhatshana	Chest, the	sehuba, dihuba
Bushman	Mosarwa	Chew, to	tlhahuna/ tlhafuna
Bustard, a	kgori	Chief, a	kgosi, dikgosi
Busy, to be	nna le tirô	Child, a little	ngwanyana,
But	mme, fa e se		banyana
Buy, to	rêka, rekile	Child	ngwana, bana
By	fa, fa go	Child, she is with	o moimana, o ithwele
By (means of)	ka		
Child, my	ngwanakê	Coney	pela
Chin	seledu	Contradict, to	ganetsa
Choke, to	beta, betile kgama, kgamile	Conquer, to	fenya, fentsê
Chop, to	rêma, remile	Consider, to	akanya, akantsê

Church	ntlo ya thuto, matlo a thutô	Consent, to	dumêla, dumetse
		Consumption	lohuba; mothama
Clap hands, to	ôpa diatla, ôpa magofi	Cook, to (with, water)	apaya, apeile
Claw, of a bird	monôtô, menôtô	Cord, a	lodi, mogala
Claw, of a beast	lonala, dinala	Cork, a	sethibô, dithibô porôpô, diporôpô
Clean	ntlê, phêpa, with Relative Pronouns	Corn	mabêlê
		Corner, a	kgôgôrôpô, segôrô
Clean, to make	ntlafatsa, ntlafaditse	Cough, to	gôtlhôla
		Count, to	bala, badile
Climb, to	pagama, pagame	Country, a	lefatshe
Cloth	khai, dikhai, letsela, matsela	Country, open	naga
		Cover, a	sekhurumêlô, sethibô
Clothes	diaparô	Cover, to	khurumêla, khurumetse; bipa, bipile
Cloud, a	leru, maru		
Coal	legala, magala	Covet	eletsa, eleditse,
Coat	baki	Cow, a	kgomo e namagadi
Cock	koko e tona-nyana, mokoko	Coward, a	legatlapa
Cold	tsididi, serame, maruru	Cows	dikgomo tse dinamagadi
Cold, I am	ke sitilwe gatsetse	Cracked, to be	phanyegile
Colour	mmala, mebala	Crawl, to	gagaba; or, abula
Come	tla, tlile	Credit, to take on	tsaya molato, sekoloto
Come here	tla kwano	Cripple, a	segôlê, digôlê
Come in	tsêna, tsenye	Crocodile	kwena, dikwena
Come out	tswa, dule	Crooked, it is	go kgopame sôkame
Come near, to	atamêla, atametse	Cross, the	mokgôrô; or, sefapaanô
Come to pass	dirafala, dirafetse	Crow, a	legakabe, magakabe
Comfort, to	gomotsa, gomoditse	Crow, to	lela, ledile

47

Coming, he is	o etla, or, o a tla	Crush, to	pitla, pitlile
Command, to	laola, laotsê	Cry, a	selelô
Command, a	taolô, ditaolô	Cry, to	lela, ledile
Compel, to	pate1e1a, pateleditse	Cure, to	fodisa, fodisitse
Complain, to	ngôngôrêga, ngô-ngôregile	Cured, to become	fôla, fodile
		Custom, a	mokgwa, mekgwa; temalô, ngwaô
Condemn, to	pega, naya molato, sekisa, sekisitse	Cup, a	kopi, dikopi
Cut off, to	kgaola, kgaotsê	Disease	bolwetsi, pobolô or botlhôko
Cut, to	sega, segile	Dish	sejana, dijana
Cut oneself, to	itshega, itshegile	Dislike, to	ila, idile
		Dispute, to	tsaya kgang
		Dispute, a	kgang, dikgang
Daily	ka malatsi otlhe	Divide, to	kgaoganya,
Damp	bokgôla bongôla, metsi	kgaogantsê	
		Divorce, to	tlhala, tlhadile
Dance, to	bina, binnê	Do, to	dira, dirile
Dark	lefifi	Do for, to serve	dirêla, diretse
Dash to pieces	phatlakanya	Doctor	ngaka, dingaka
Dawn	bosa; mahube	Doctor, to	alafa, alafile
Day	letsatsi, malatsi; to-day, gompieno	Dog	ntša, dintša
		Door	setswalô, ditswalô lebati, mabati
Daylight	motshegare	Doubt, to	belaêla, belaetse
Dead, he is	o sule	Dove, a	lephoi, maphoi leeba, maeba
Deaf, he is	o bosusu	Down, below	kwa teng, ka kwa tlase
Death	loso		
Debt	molato, melato	Draw, to	gôga,
Decay, to	bôla, bodile; senyêga	(drag or pull)	gogile
		Dream, to	lôra, lorile
Deceive, to	tsietsa, taieditse	Dress, to	apara, apere

48

December	Morule	Drink, to	nwa, nolê
Deep	boteng	Drive, to	kgweetsa, kgweeditse
Defeat, to	fenya, fentsê	Drunk, to be	tagilwe
Defend, to	femêla, femetse	Drunk, to make	tagwa, tagilwe
Delay, to cause	dia, diile; to tarry, diêga,	Dry, to become	ôma, omile
Deny, to	itatola, itatotsê	Dry, up, as a tree	ômêlêla, omeletse
Desert, a	sekaka	Dry, to make	omisa, omisitse; omeletsa, omeleditse
Deserve	tshwanetse		
Desolate, to become	swafala, swafetse	Dry up, to, as water	kgala, kga dite; tšha, tšhelê
Despise, to	nyatsa, nyaditse	Duck	sehudi, dihudi
Destroy, to	senya, sentsê	Dumb, he is	o semumu
Destroyed, to become	senyêga, senyegile	Dung (wet)	bolôkô
Die, to	swa, sule	Dust	lorole, dithole
Difficult, it is	go thata	Duster	sephimolô
Dig, to	êpa, epile	Dust, to	phimola, phimotsê
Dip, to	ina, innê	Duiker, a	photi, diphoti
Dirt	mabebe, or, malele	Dysentery	taboga madi (mala a mahubidu)
Dirty	leswê		
Eagle, an	ntswi, ntsu	Eye, to open	budulola
Ear, an	tsêbê, ditsêbê	Eye, to close	budulatsa
Early	go sa le galê		
Earth, the	lefatshe		
Easy	bofefo, botlhôfo		
Easy, to take it	iketla	Fable, a	tlhamane
Eat, to	ja, jelê	Face	sefatlhêgô
Egg, an	lee, mae	Faint, to; he has fainted	idibala; o idibetse,
Eland, an	phohu, diphohu		
Elbow	sekgono	Fall, to	go wa; o olê, he has fallen
Elephant, an	tlou, ditlou		
Embrocation	setlôlô	Fall into	wêla mo

49

Empty	ga go na sepê, lolea	Famine	leuba
		Fan, to	go bôka;ipôka, to fan oneself
End, the	bokhutlô		
End, to bring to	khutlisa	Fan, a	kaba, dikaba
Enemy	mmaba, baba	Far, it is	go kgakala
		Fast, to	itima dijô
English	Sekgowa	Fasten, to	hunêla, bôfa,
Enough, it is	go lekanye		funêla
Enquire, to	botsa, boditse	Fat	mahura
Envious	pelotshêtlha	Fat, he is	o nônnê
Equal	lekalekanye	Father	rra, rrê, rara, ntate
Escape, to	falola, falotsê	Fault	molato
Establish, to confirm	tlhômamisa	Fear	poifô
		Fear, to	boifa, boifile
Established, to be	tlhomame	Feast	modirô, medirô
Eternal	ka bosakhutleng, ka bosayengkae	Feather	lofafa, diphofa
		February	Tlhakolê
Evening	maitsibowa	Feed, to	jesa, jesitse
Everywhere	ntlheng tsotlhe	Feel, to	utlwa
Evidence	tshupô, paki	Fence, a	logora, dikgora
Evidence, to give	supa, paka	Fever	mogote,or letshoroma, malarial fever
Evil	bosula		
Example	sekaô, sekai	Fight, to	lwa, lolê, tlhabana, tlhabanye
Excel, to	gaisa, gaisitse		
Except	fa e se	Fill, to	tlatsa, tladitse; it is full, go tletse
Exchange, to	ananya, anantsê		
Excite, to	gakatsa	Find, to	bôna, bonye, fitlhêla, fitlhetse
Excited, to be	gaketse		
Excuse, an	seipatô, diipatô	Finger	monwana, menwana
Expect, to	lebêlêla, lebeletse; ke lebeletse, I expect.	Finish, to	fetsa, feditse, swetsa, sweditse
Eye	leitlhô, matlhô	Finished, to be	fedile
Fire	molelô, melelô	Fruit, to bear	ungwa, ungwile

Fireplace	leisô, maisô	Fortunate, he is	o segô
Fire, to set on	tshuba, tshubile	Future	kwa pele, lobaka
Fire, to light	gotsa		lo lo tlang
First	ntlha, with possessive pronouns	Full	tletse
Fish	tlhapi, ditlhapi		
Fist	letswele, mabole		
Fix, to	tlhôma, baakanya	Game	diphôlôgôlô
Flame, a	kgabo, dikgabo	Garden, a	tshimo, masimo
Flat	papetla	Gargle, to	itsukula
Flee, to	tshaba, tshabile	Gather, to	phutha, phuthile
Flee to, to	tshabêla kwa, or kwa go	Gather, fruit, to	fula loungô
		Get, to	bôna, bonye
Float, to	kokobala	Gift, a	nêô, mphô
Flow, to	êla, eletse	Giraffe, a	thutlwa, dithutlwa
Flower	tšheše, ditšheše, sethunya, dithunya	Girl	mosetsana, basetsana
		Give to, to	naya, neile;fa, file
Flower, to	thunya, thuntsê	Give away, to	aba, abile
Fly, a	ntsi, dintsi	Give money, etc,to	ntsha madi, ntshitse madi
Fly, to	fofa, fofile	Give back, to	busa, busitse
Foal	pêtsana	Give food, to	fa, file; give me,
Fold, to	mena, mennê		mpha
Follow, to	sala moragô, latêla, latetse	Give care of, to	nêêla, neetse
Food	sejô, dijô	Glad, to be	itumêla, itumetse
Fool, a	lesilo, masilo	Gladness	boitumêlô
Foolishness	boeleele, bohephela	Glory	kgalalêlô
Foot	lonao, dinao kgatô, dikgatô	Gnu	kgokong, dikgokong
Forbid, to	itsa, iditse	Go, to	ya, ile
Forest	sekgwa, dikgwa	Go away, to	tsamaya, tsamaile
Forget, to	lebala, lebetse	Go back	boêla kwa moragô
Forgive, to	itshwarêla, itshwaretse	Go down, to	fologa
		Go in, to	tsêna, tsenye

Form, to	bopa, bopile	Go on, to	tswêlêla,
Fountain	motswedi,		tsweletse
	metswedi	Go out, to	tswa, dule
Fowl, a	koko, dikoko	Goat	podi, dipodi
Friend, a	tsala, ditsala	God	Modimo
Friendly with, to be,	tsalana le, tsalanye le	Good	molemo; he is good, o molemô
Frighten, to	tshosa, tshositse	Goods	dilwana, thoto
Frock	mosese, mesese	Gospel	Efangele
Fruit	loungô (collective)	Govern, to	busa, busitse
Government	mmusô, pusô	Hat, put on	rwala hutshe
Grace	tshegofatsô, letlhôgônôlô	Hate, to	tlhôa, tlhôile
		Hawk, a	segodi and segootsane, phakalane
Grapes	moretlwa		
Grass	bojang, majang	Head	tlhôgô, ditlhôgô
Grave, a	phupu, lebitla	Headache	ôpiwa ke tlhôgô
Great	kgolo, golo, tonna, with relative pronoun	Headman	mogolwane, kgôsana
		Heap, a	mokoa, mekoa
Green	tala	Heal, to	fodisa, fodisitse
Greet, to	dumedisa, dumedisitse	Healed, to become	fola, fodile
Grope	apaapa	Hear, to	utlwa, utlwile
Ground, on the	fa fatshe	Heart	pelo, dipelo
Grind, to	sila, sidile	Heat	bothithô, mogote
Grow, to	gola, godife	Heaven	legodimo, magodimo
Grumble, to	ngôngôrêga	Heavy	bokete
Guard, to	lebêla, disa	Hedge, a	logora, dikgora
Guineafowl	kgaka, dikgaka	Heel	serêthê, dirêthê
Gun	tlhôbôlô, ditlhôbôlô	Heifer, a	kgomo ya moroba
Gunpowder	mosidi	Help, to	thusa, thusitse
Guide, a	mosupatsela	Help	thusô
Guilty, he is	o molato	Helper	mothusi, bathusi
Gum	boroku	Hen, a	koko e namagadi
Gums, the	marinini or mahinini	Herdboy, a	modisa, badisa
		Herd, to	disa, disitse

Habit, a	mokgwa, têmalô	Here	fa, fano, mono
Had, he had	o ne a na le	Hide, to	suba, fitlha, lôba, subile, fitlhile, lobile
Hail	sefakô	Hide, a	letlalô, matlalô
Hair	moriri	Hidden	subegile, fitlhegile, lôbafetse
Hammer	nôtô, dinôtô		
Hand	seatla, diatla	High	godimo
Hang, up to	pêga, pegile	Hill	lentswê, majê; thota, dithota
Happy, to be	itumêla, itumetse		
		Him	mo (m, before verb)
Happy, he is	o itumetse		
Hard	thata	Hinder, to	kgoreletsa, kgoreleditse
Hare	mmutla, mebutla		
Has and have	na le; he has a knife:o na le thipa	Hip	nôka
		Hit, to	itaya, iteile;
		Hither	kwano
Haste, to make	akofa, nanoga, itlhaganêlê	Hoax, to	fora, forile
Hat	hutshe, dihutshe	Hold fast, to	tshegetsa, tshegeditse, tshwara, tshwere thata
Hat, take off	rola hutshe		
Hold, to take	tshwara, tshwere	Inside out, to turn	tlhanola, tlhanotsê
Hole, in cloth,	leroba, maroba		
		Injure, to	gobatsa, gobaditse
Hole, in ground	lehuti, mahuti		golafala, golafetse
Hole, in a tree	letshwagô, matshwagô		
		Interpret, to	tolokolola tolokolotse
Hole, made by animal in ground	mosima, mesima	Iron	tshipi, ditshipi
		Iron, to	sola, sodile; gatisa, gatisitse
Holiness	boitshêpô	Irritate, to	baba, babalêla
		Is, is expressed by the pronominal particles, *e.g., 0 montlê,*	

53

Hollow, a	khuti, dikhuti, lehuti, mahuti,legapa		She is pretty; ba mono, they
Holy	itshêpa		are here; di
Home	legae; at home, kwa gae		maswê, they are bad, etc.
Honey	dinotshe	Is it she?	a ke ênê?
Honour, to	tlotla, tlotlile		
		Is it right?	a go siame?
Hoof	tlhako, ditlhako	Is not	ga, with the pronouns:
Hope	tsholofêlô		ga a montlê, she is not pretty;
Hope, to	solofêla, solofetse		ga a yô, he is not here
Horn	lonaka, dinaka	It was with nouns	e ne e le,
Hornet, a	moruthwane		and pronouns; go ne go le,
Horse	pitse, dipitse		with adjectives
		It will be	e tla a nna, *and*
Hot	mogote, molelô		go tla a nna
House	ntlo, mantlo	It is	ke, with nouns and pronouns;-
How?	jang?		ke ênê, it is he; ke bônê,
How long?	ka lobaka lo lo kaye?		it is they; ke kgomo, it is an ox
Hunger	tlala, logaba		
Hungry, to be	bolailwe ke tlala	It is	go, with adjectives, go
Hunt, to	tsoma, tsomile		bosula, it is bad; go botlhoko,
Hurt, to	utlwisa botlhoko		it is bitter; go ntse jalo, it is so
Husband	monna, banna	It is not	ga se, and ga go;
Hyena	phiri, diphiri		ga se ênê it is not he; ga go bosula, it is not bad; it is not so, ga

If	fa, e re fa		go a nna jalo
Impossible, it is	go retetse	I	ke, nna
In	mo, with ng at	Island, an	setlhakatlhake,
	end of nouns		setlhake
	or, mo go, before		ditlhakatlhake
	names of persons		
	and pronouns	Itch, to	baba, babile
Increase	loatô, kôkêtsêgô	Ivory	lonaka lwa tlou
Increase, to	ata, atile; ôkêtsêga		
Inside	mo teng, kwa teng		
Inspan, to	golêga, golegile		
Instead, of	mo boemong jwa		
Jackal	phokojê, tlhose		
Jackal, silver	phokojê, diphokojê		
January	Ferikgong	Labour, work	tirô
Jealous, he is	o pelotshêtlha	Labourer	modiri
Jealousy	lefufa	Lack, to	tlhôka, tlhokile
Join, to	kôpanya,	Ladder, a	lere, sepagamô
	kôpantsê		
Join with, to	kôpana le	Lady, a	mohumagadi
Joint	lelokololô,	Lake	bodiba, letšha
	lekônô		
Journey, to	êta, etile	Lamb	kwanyana
Journey, a	loêtô, maêtô	Lame, he is	o a tlhotsa
Justify, to	siamisa	Lamp	lobônê
Joy	boitumêlô	Land	lefatshe
Judge, to	atlhola, atlhotsê	Language	puô, dipuô
Judge, a	moatlhodi	Large	golo, kgolo, tona
Judgement	katlholô	Last, the	bofêlô, with
			possessive
July	Phukwi		pronouns
Jump, to	tlola, tlodile	Laugh, to	tshêga, tshegile
June	Seêtêbosigo	Laugh, a	setshêgô,
			ditshêgô
Just so	le galê	Laugh, to	bolaisa ditshêgô
Just, he is	o siame	make to	
Just, he is not	ga a a siama	Law	molaô, melaô
Justice	tshiamô	Lay, to	baya, beile
Lazy	bobodu,	Lead, to	gôga, gogile
	botshwakga		

55

Kaross, a	kobô, dikobô	Leaf	letlhare, matlhare
Keep, to	boloka, bolokile, baya, beile	Leak, to	dutla, dutlile
Kick, to	raga, ragile	Lean	mokôgô (bopama)
Kidney	philô, diphilô	Lean, on to	ikaêga
Kill, to	bolaya, bolaile	Learn, to	ithuta, ithutile
Kindness	bobelonomi	Leave, to	tlogêla, tlogetse
King	kgosi, dikgosi	Leaven	sebedisô
Kingdom	bogosi, magosi	Leaven, to	bedisa, bedisitse
Kiss, to	atla, suna	Leg	leoto, maoto
Kloof, a	kgôrô, phata	Leg, of meat	serope
Knead, to	duba, dubile	Lend, to	adima, adimile
Knee	lengôlê, mangôlê	Let	mma, a; mma ke yê, let me go; a re tsamayeng, let us go
Knife	thipa, dithipa		
Knock, to	kôkôta, kokonya		
Knot	lehutô, mahutô	Letter, a	lokwalô, dikwalô
Know, to	itse, itsile	Liar, a	moaki, baaki
Knowledge	kitsô	Lick, to	latswa, latswitse
Koorhaan, a	tlatlawê, botlatlawê	Lie, to	aka, akile
		Lie, to,(sleep)	go lala, letse
Kraal	lesaka, maraka	Lie down	rapama, rapame
Lies	maaka	Man	monna, banna
Life	botshelô	Many	ntsi, with prefixes
Lift, to	tsholetsa, tsholeditse	Many people	batho ba bantsi
Light weight	motlhofo	March	Mopitlô
Light	lesedi, masedi	Mark, a brand	lotshwaô
Lightning	logadima, tladi	Mark, to brand	tshwaya, tshwaile
Like, to	rata, ratile		
Like, to be	tshwana, tshwana le	Marry, to	tsaya, tsere; nyala, nyetse
Line, a	thapô, moralô		
Lion, a	tau, ditau	Married legally, to be	êma, eme nyala, or nyalwa
Lip, a	pounama, dipounama	Marry, to, to officiate	emisa, nyadisa, emisitse
Listen, to	reetsa, reeditse	Master	mong, beng
Little, a	go le gonnye	Mat, a	phatê, moalô
Little, he is	o monnye	May	Motsheganong
Live, to	tshela, tshedile		

Live, to dwell	aga, agile	Me	m, or, n, prefixed
Liver	sebete		to verb
Load, a	morwalô	Meal	boupe, bopi
Lock, a	selôtô	Measure, to	lekanya, lekantsê
Lock, to	kôpêla, lôtlêla	Measure, a	selekanyô
Locusts	tsiê	Meat	nama, dinama
		Meat, to cut	gôlôla, golotse
		up for drying,	
Long	leele, telele;	Medicine	molemô, melemô
	with prefixes	Meet,	phuthêga,
Long ago	bogologolo	together	phuthegile
Look at, to	leba, lebile	Meet with	kgatlhana le
Looking-glass	seipone	Melon	lekatane,
Lord	Morêna		makatane
Lost, to be	go latlhêga	Melon, water	legapu, magapu
	is lost,latlhegile;	Melon,	kgêngwê
	I have lost,	wild bitter	
	ke latlhegetswe	Melt to	gakolosa,
			tlhapolosa
Louse	nta, dinta	Mend, to	baakanya,
Love	loratô		baakantsê
Love, to	rata, ratile	Mercy	boutlwêlô-
			botlhôko
Lucky	segô; he is	Mercy, to	utlwêla bo tlhoko
	lucky, o segô	have	
Lung	lekgwafo,	Mid-day	motshegare,
	makgwafo		sethôbôlôkô
		Milk	maši, lebese
Mad person	setsênwa	Milk, sour	madila
Madness	botsênwa	Milk, to	gama, gamile
Maggot	seboko, diboko	Milk-sack, a	lekuka, makuka
Maize	mmidi, or mmopo	Mill, a	lelwala, malwala
			tshilô, ditshilô
Make, to	dira, dirile	Mind, to	disa, tlhôkômêla,
			bôna, êlatlhôkô
Mine, a	mokoti, mekoti	Narrow	sesane, tshesane
Minister, a	moruti, baruti	Near	gaufi, gaufi le
Mirage	meênênê;meeledi	Neck	thamo, dithamo;
Miss, a	phosô		molala, melala
Miss, to	fosa, fositse	Needle	lomaô, dimaô
Mistake, a	timêlô, phôsô	Nest	sentlhaga,

Misty	looto		dintlhaga
Mist	mouwane	Net	lotloa, matloa
	moiwane	Never	gopê, ka gopê
Mix, to	tlhakanya,	Nevertheless	le fa go ntse jalo
	tlhakantsê	New	ntšha, seša, with
Mixed up, to be	tlhakanye		Relative
Pronouns			
Mock, to	sotla, tlaopa	News	mafoko, dikgang
Money	madi, šhêlêtê		
Monkey	kgabo, dikgabo		
Month	kgwedi,		
	dikgwedi	Nice	monate, molemô
Moon	kgwedi (ngwedi)	Night	bosigo, masigo
Moonlight, it is	go ngwedi	No	nnya, nnyaa
Morning, this	phakêla,mosô	Noise, a	modumô, leratla
	ono		
Mosquito	montsana,	Noise, to	tsosa modumô,
	monang	make	tlhodia
Most	bogolo	Nose	nkô, dinkô
Mother	mma; mmê, my	Nor	ga, ga, se, sa, e
	mother		seng
Motion, have	a o ile ntlê?	Nothing, it is	ga se sepê
you had a?	a o ile kgôrong?	Notice	kitsisô, tlhagisô
Mouse, a	pêba, dipêba	Notice, to	itsise
Mouth	molomo, melomo	give	
Mouth, to open	atlhama,	November	Ngwanatsêlê
	atlhame	Now	jaanong, jaana
Move, to	suta, sutile	Nowhere	gopê
Move, to, cause	sutisa	Number	palô
to		Number, to	bala, dira palô
Much	thata	Numbness	bogatsu
Mud	serêtsê	Nurse, to	ôka, okile; amusa,
Muscle	mosifa, mesifa		amusitse
Multiply, to	ntsifatsa	Nurse, a	moamusi,
			baamusi
			mooki, baoki
Nail	lomapô, dimapô	Oath, to take	ikana, ikannê
	sepekere,	Oath, an	ikanô, maikanô
	dipekere		
Nail, finger/toe	lonala, dinala	Obey, to	utlwa

Name	leina, maina	Observe, to	tlhôkômêla
Name, to	raya leina	Obstinate	logwadi, logwane
Nasty	maswê	October	Phalane
Offend, to	kgopisa, kgopisitse	Parcel, a	ngata, dingata
Offering	tshupêlô	Pardon, to	itshwarêla,
Often	gantsi, gantsintsi		itshwaretse
Oil	lookwane, wele	Pardon	boitshwarêlô
Ointment	setlôlô	Parliament	Palamente
Old	bogologolo, with Possessive Pronouns	Part, a	ntlha nngwe
		Partridge	lesogo, masogo
Olive tree	motlhware	Party, a	lesomô, lekôkô
On	mo, fa, mo go, fa go	Pass, a	kgôrô, dikgôrô
Once, only	gangwe fêla	Pass (permit)	pasa, dipasa
One	nngwe, with Prefixes	Pass by, to	feta, fetile
Only	fêla	Past	mo go fetileng
Open, to	bula, budile	Patch a	sebata, dibata
Open, it is	go bulegile, go budilwe	Patch, to	bitia, bitietse
		Path	tsela, ditsela
Opening, an	kgôrô, dikgôrô	Patience	bobelotelele
Openly	fa pele ga batho	Pattern, a	sekaô, dikaô
Opposite, to	lebaganye le	Pay, to	duêla, duetse
Or	kgotsa, le fa e le	Pay	tuêlô, kamogêlô
Order, to	laola, laotsê	Paw	leroo, maroo
Ore	borale	Peace	kagisô
Orphan	lesiêla, khutsana	Peace, to make	agisa, agisitse, letlanya, letlantsê
Ostrich	ntšhe, bontšhe		
Ought	tshwanetse	Pen	pene, or, sekwadi
Ought not	ga go a tshwanêla	Pencil	pôtlôlôtô
Outside	kwa ntlê, ka fa ntlê	People	batho
Outspan	golola, golotsê	Perfect, tense	mo go setseng go fedile
Oven	pesetso	Perfect, to be	itekanêla, itekanetse
Overcome, to	fenya, fentsê sita, sitile	Perhaps	kgotsa; kampo,

Owe, to	molato le, kolota		gongwe
Owl	morubisi	Permit, to	lesa, lesitse
Ox	pholo, dipholo	Persevere, to	tswêlêla pele, itshôka, itshokile
Pain, in heart or chest	setlhabi, ditlhabi	Person, a	motho, batho
		Perspiration	mofufutsô
Pain	botlhoko	Perspire, to	fufula, fufutsê
Pain, to cause	tlhokofatsa, or utlwisa botlhoko	Pick a	peke, dipeke
		Pick, to	peka, pekile; êpa, epile ka peke
Pain, to feel	go utlwa botlhoko		
Parable, a	setshwantshô, ditshwantshô	Piece, a	kabetla, sebata
		Pierce, to	phunya, phuntsê
Pierced, to become	phunyêga, phunyegile	Praise, to	baka, bakile; bôka, bokile
Pig	kolobê, dikolobê	Pray, to	rapêla, rapetse
Pigeon	leeba, maeba	Prayer, a	thapêlô
		Pray for, to	rapêlêla,rapeletse
Pillow, a	mosamô, mesamô	Pray, let us	a re rapeleng
Pillow, to put	sama, samile	Pregnant	moimana
Pinch, to	ngapa, ngapile	Prepare, to	baakanya, baakantsê
Pit	petse,kgatlampi		
Plain, a	poana, dipoana	Present, a	nêô, mphô
Place, a	felô, lefelô, golo	Present, time	jaanong jaana
Place, to	baya, beile	Presently	kgantelê
Plait, to	loga, logile	Press, to	gatisa, gatisitse
Plans, to make	loga maanô	Pretty	ntlê, with prefixes
Plant, to	tlhôma; lema	Price	tlhwatlhwa
Plant, a	setlhatshana	Prick, to	tlhaba, tlhabile
Play	tshamekô	Pride	mabela; makama
Play, to	tshameka; raloka	Prince, a	morwa kgosi
Play an instrument	letsa, leditse; tshameka diletswa	Prison	kgolêgêlô
		Proper, it is	go siame, go lebanye
Plead, to	rapêla, rapetse	Proud	mabela
Please	a ko o, a ko lo, before the Verb, tswêêtswêê	Provide for, to	tlamêla, tlametse
Please, to	kgatlha, kgatlhile	Puffadder	lebolobolo
Pleased, I am	ke itumetse	Pull	gôga, gagamatsa; gogile, gagamaditse
Plough, a	mogoma, megoma		

Plough, to	lema, lemile	Pumpkin	lephutshe
Plug, to	kaba, kabile	Punish, to	betsa; ôtlhaa
Plural	bobedi; bontsi	Pure, is	itshekile; ntlê; phêpa
Point, a	ntlha, dintlha	Pure, to make	itshekisa
Point, to	supa, supile	Purge, to	tshabisa, tshabisitse
Poison	botlhôle; more	Purged, to be	taboga mo maleng
Pole, a	mopakô, mepakô		
Polish, to	gotlha, or, sutlha	Pus	boladu
Pool, in a river	bodiba	Push	kgarametsa; kgorometsa
Poor, I am	ke humanegile		
Porcupine	noko, dinoko	Put (to place)	baya, beile
Porridge	bogôbê		
Pot, a	pitsa, dipitsa		
Pot, a small	pitsana	Quarrel, to	ômana, ômanye
Potato, a	lekwele, makwele	Quarrel, a	kgang, kgotlhang
Pour, to	tshêla, tshetse	Queen	mohumagadi
Powder	loupe, boupe	Quench fire	tima, timile
		Remind to	gakolola, gakolotsê
Question, a	potsô, dipotsô		
Question, to	botsa, boditse	Remove to	tlosa, tlositse
Quickly	ka bonakô/bofefo	Remove residence	huduga, hudugile
Quiet, to be	didimala, didimetse		
Quiet, to make	didimatsa	Repent, to	ikwatlhaya
Quietly	ka tidimalô	Reply, to	araba, arabile
Quince	kupere, dikupere	Reprove, to	ômanya, ômantsê
Quite	ruri, preceded by Verb ending in -êla	Rest	tapologô; boikhutsô
		Rest, to	itapolosa, itapolositse
		Rested, to be	lapologile; lapologetswe
		Return, to	bowa, boile
		Return, to cause to	busa, busitse
Rabbit, a rock	pela, dipela		
Rafter, a	tlhomeso	Reveal to	senola, senotsê
Rag, a	sekatana, dikatana	Rich, to be	humile
Rain	pula	Ride, to	pagama, pagame

Rainpool — mogobe, megobe

Rainbow — motshe wa badimo

Rains, it — pula e a na, e nelê

Rash, a — mokwana

Rash, to come out, in a — rokomologa, rokomologile

Read, to — bala, badile;

Ready, to make — baakanya, baakantsê

Ready, I am — ke ipaakantsê

Rear, to, of horse — kwela

Rebuke, to — ômanya, ômantsê

Receive, to — amogêla, amogetse

Recline — rapama, rapame

Reconcile, to — letlanya, letlantsê

Recover, to, from sickness — fôla, fodile; sidilêga

Red — khibidu; khubidu

Redeem, to — rekolola, rekolotsê

Reed — lotlhaka, ditlhaka

Refuse, to — gana, gannê

Rejoice, to — itumêla, itumetse; ipela, ipetse

Release, to — golola, golotsê

Remain, to — sala, setse

Remember, to — gakologêlwa, gakologetswe

Rust — rusi, or, morodi

Rusty — rusitse

Sabbath — Sabata

Sack, a — kgetse, dikgetse

Saddle — sale

Safe, it is — go bolokegile

Safe, to be — go bolokegile

Ridge, of country — lerôpô, lekwelekwele

Riem — kgôlê, dikgôlê

Right — tshiamô, tshiamêlô

Right, it is — go siame

Ring, to — letsa, leditse

Rinse out, to — tsokotsa, tsokoditse

Ripe, to be — budule

Ripe, to become — butswa

Rise, to — tsoga, tsogile

River — noka, dinoka; molapô, melapô

Road — tsela, ditsela

Roast, to — besa, besitse

Rock — lefika, mafika;

Rock, a flat — letlapa, matlapa

Rogue, a — leferefere, maferefere

Root — modi

Rot, to — bôla, bodile

Rub, to, massage — sedila, seditse

Rub, to, to clean — gotlha, gotlhile, sutlha, sutlhile

Run, to — siana,,sianye; taboga, tabogile

Run, out-run — sia, siile

Sell, to — rekisa, rekisitse; bapatsa, bapaditse

Send, to (person) — roma, romile

Send for, to — romêla, rometse

Send away, to — lêlêka, lelekile, koba, kobile

Send a thing, to — isa, isitse

62

Salt	letswai	September	Lwetse
Saltpan, a	letšha, matšha	Servant	motlhanka,
Salvation, active:	poloka;		batlhanka
passive:	polokô	Servant, maid	lelata, malata
Sand, river	mošawa	Serve, to	dirêla, diretse
Satisfied (food)	kgotshe	Sew, to	roka, rokile
Save, to	boloka, bolokile	Shade	moruti, meruti
Saviour	Mmoloki	Shake, to	tshikhinya,
Say, to	re, rile		tshikhintsê
Say to, to	raya, reile	Shake,	tshikhinyêga
Scab, a	logôgô, dikgôgô		(passive)
Scales	sekale	Shake, to,	udubatsa,
Scald, to	fisa, fisitse	(carpet)	udubaditse
Scar	lobadi, dipadi	Shall	tla a
		Shame	ditlhong, kgala
		Sharp	bogale
Scatter, to	falatsa, faladitse	Sharpen, to	lootsa, looditse
Scattered, to be	faletse	Shed, a	loôbô, maôbô
Scissors	sekêrê	Sheep	nku, dinku
Scold, to	kgalemêla,	Shine, to	phatsima,
	kgalemetse		phatsimile
		Shine, to	phatsimisa,
Scorch, to	babola, babotsê	cause to	phatsimisitse
Scorpion	phepheng,	Shirt	hêmpê, dihêmpê
	diphepheng	Shiver, to	roroma; têtêsêla
Scrape, to	fala, fadile	Shoe	setlhako, ditlhako
Scratch, to	ngwaya, ngwaile	Shoe, to	rwala, rwele
		put on	(with setlhako)
Scream, to	gala, gadile	Shoe, to	
Sea	lewatlê, mawatlê	take off	rola, rotsê
Search for, to	senka, senkile	Shoot, to	go fula, fudile;
			thuntsha
			(tlhôbôlô)
Secretary, a	mokwaledi	Short	khutshwane
See, to	bôna, bonye	Shot, small	marumô,
			masesane
Seed	peo, dipeo	Shoulder	legetla, magetla
Seed, a grain of	tlhaka	Shoulder	legôpê
		blade	
Seek, to	batla, batlile;	Shout, to	goa, goile; kua,
	senka, senkile		kuile

Select, to	tlhaola, tlhaotsê	Shout, after	tlhaeletsa
Show to	supa, supile	Snatch, to	phamola,
Show, to, to	supetsa		phamotsê
	supeditse	Snuff	motsoko wa
Shut, to	tswala, tswetse		dinkô
Sick, to be	bobola, or, lwala,	So	jalo, jaana
	nna botlhôko	Soap	molôra
Side	ntlha, dintlha	Soft	bonôlô, bolêta,
Side of a	lotlhakore,		boruma
person	mofama	Softly	ka bonôlô
Silent, to be	didimala, didime-	Soldier, a	motlhabani,
	tse, tuulala,		batlhabani,
	tuuletse		lesôlê, masôlê
		Son	morwa, bomorwa,
		ngwana wa mosimane,	
		bana ba basimane, barwa	
Sin	boleo, maleo,	Soon	kgantelê
	sebe, dibe	Sore, a	nthô, dinthô
Sinew	losika, ditshika,	Sore, to be	botlhoko
	mosifa, mesifa	Sorrow	bohutsana
Sing, to	ôpêla, opetse	Sorry, to be	utlwa botlhoko,
			hutsafala
Sing, let us	a re opeleng	Soul	mowa, mewa
Singular	bongwe fêla	Soup	morô
Sit, to	dula, dutsê;	Sour	botlha
	nna, ntse	South	borwa
Skim off, to	okola, okotsê	Sow, to	jala, jadile; jwala,
Skin	letlalô, matlalô		jwetse
Skin, to	go bua letlalô	Spark	tlhase, ditlhase
Slaughter, to	tlhaba, tlhabile	Speak, to	bua, buile
Sleep	borôkô	Spear	lerumô, marumô
Sleep, to	rôbala, robetse;	Speech	puô, dipuô
	o robetse, he	Spider, a	segokgo, digokgo
	is asleep	Spirit	mowa, mewa
Sleepy, to be	otsêla	Spit, to	kgwa mathe
Slip, to	rêlêla, reletse	Splinter, a	phatsa, diphatsa
Slippery	borethe	Split, to	fatsa, fatola,
Slow	bonya		fatotsê, fatsitse
Slowly	ka bonya	Split, it is	go fatogile
Small	pôtlana, nnye	Spoil, to	senya, sentsê; is
Small-pox	sekgwaripane		spoiled,

64

			o senyegile
Smell, a	monkô, monkgô	Spoon	lesô, dintshô
Smell, a savoury	lonkô	Spoor	motlhala,metlhala
Smell, to emit, a	nkga	Sports	metshamekô
Smell, anything, to	dupa, dupêlêla	Sprained	phethegile, sonyegile
Smith, a	mothudi, bathudi	Spring	Dikgakologô
Smoke	mosi	Spread (cloth)	ala, adile
Smoke, a pipe,to	gôga, peipa, tsuba	Spread, as roots	anama
Smooth	borethe	Springbok	tshêphê
Snake	nôga, dinôga	Sprinkle, to	kgatšha, kgatšhitse
Staff, a	lore, dinthe, thôbane dithôbane	Stupid	bosilo, seefeele
		Suck (of mouth)	mona, momonnê
Stamp corn, to	tlhobola, thuga mabêlê		
Stamping,	kika le motshe block and pestle	Suck, to, (breast)	anya, amule
Stand, cause to	emisa	Suck, to give	amusa, amusitse
Stand, to	êma, eme; he is standing, O eme	Suddenly Summer	ka tshoganetso Selemô
Star	naledi, dinaledi	Sun, the	letsatsi
Startle, to	tshosa, tshositse	Sunday	Tshipi, Sôntaga
Startled, to be	tshogile	Sunrise	tlhabô ya letsatsi
		Sunset	phirimô ya letsatsi
Starve, to	bopama, bopame bolawa ke tlala	Surround, to	dikanyetsa,
Stay a day, to	tlhôla, tlhotse		dika, dikile
Stay a night, to	lala, letse	Suspect, to	belaêla
Steal, to	utswa, utswile	Swallow, a	peolwane, dipeo-
Steinbuck	phuduhudu		lwane (peolane, dipeolane)
Stick, a	thupa, dithupa	Swallow, to	metsa, meditse;
Stick, a dry	logong, dikgong		kodumetsa,
Stick, to	ngaparêla, kgomarêla		kodumeditse
		Swallow up, to	kometsa,
Stick, cause to	ngaparetsa, kgomaretsa		komeditse

65

Still, to be	nna fêla, ntse fêla tuulala, sisibala	Swear and curse, to	roga, rogile, rogaka; rogakana
Stir, to	hudua, huduile	Swear, (to take an oath)	ikana, ikannê
Stomach	mala, mpa, mogodu		
Stone, a	lentswê, majê	Sweep, to	fêêla, feetse
Stop (to cease)	khutla, khutlile	Swept	feetswe
Stop, to	kganêla, kganetse	Sweet	botshe; monate wa tatsô
	êma, emisa	Swell, to	ruruga, rurugile
Straight	siame, lolame	Swelling, a	thurugô
Straight, to make	siamisa, tlhamalatsa	Swift, to be	fefoga, fefogile
Strain, to	tlhôtlha, tlhotlhile	Swim, to	šapa; thuma; tunka
Stranger, a	moeng, baeng	Swinging, to be	akgêga akgegile
Stray, to	timêla, timetse	Swoon, to	ngatêga,
Street	mmila, mebila		gonoga
Stretch tightly, to	gagamatsa, ff, ngamola	Sword	tšhaka, ditšhaka
		Table	lomati (or lobati)
Stretched, to be	gagametse		lwa bojêlô
Strife	kgang, dikgang	Tail	mogatla, megatla
Strike, to	itaya, iteile, ditaya, diteile	Take, to	tsaya, tseile, tshola
String, a	mogala	Take to, to	isa, isitse, *with*
Strong	thata; nonofile		kwa, or kwa go if before name
Stump, a	sesana, disana		of person or Pronoun
Take away	tlosa; tsaya	To, towards	kwa; kwa go
Talk, to	bua, buile	Tobacco	motsoko, metsoko
Tangled, to be	raraanye	To-day	gompieno; ka jeko
Taste, to	utlwa; leka ka leganô; utlwelêla	Toe	monwana wa lenao
Tax	lekgêthô	Together	mmôga
Tax, to	kgethisa	To-morrow	ka mosô
Tax, gatherer	mokgethisi	Tongue	loleme, diteme, maleme
Teach, to	ruta, rutile		
Teacher	moruti, baruti	Too much	bobe; go go
Tears	dikeledi		tona bobe, it is
Tear, to	gagola, gagotsê		too much; go

Tease, to	tshwenya, tshwentsê		gonnye bobe, it is too little
Teat	letsêlê; lebêlê	Tooth	leinô, mênô
Telegraph	mogala, megala	Toothache	motlhagare, or,
Telegraph office	ntlo ya mogala		bolawa ke mênô
Telegraph, to	itaya mogala, iteile mogala	Top, the	godimo
		Tortoise	khudu
Tell, to	bolêla, boletse	Touch, to	ama, amile
Tell, to a person	bolêlêla boleletse	Towel	sephimolô; toulô
		Town	motse, metse
Thank, to	leboga, lebogile	Trap, a	serai, dirai;selaga
That, so that	gore	Trap, to set	thaya, thaile
Thatch, to	rulêla, ruletse	Travel, to	êta, etile
Thick	kima, kgaraga	Tread, to	gata, gatile
		Tree	setlhare, ditlhare
		Tremble	roroma, têtêsêla
		Trial	tekô, ditekô; tshêkô
Thief	legodu, magodu	Tribe	setšhaba,
Thigh	serope, dirope		ditšhaba
Thin	sesane, tshesane	Tried in	go lekwa;
Thing	selô, dilô	court, to be	sekisiwa
Think, to	gopola; akanya	Trouble	tlalêlô
Thirsty	nyorilwe, bolailwe ke lenyôra	Trouble, to be in	tlaletswe pitlagane
Thought	mogopolô	Truly	ruri
Tie, to	funêla, funetse	Trunk	thitô
Tie together, to	hunaganya, hunagantsê	Trust, to	ikanya; tshêpha
		Truth	boammaaruri;
Tiger	nkwê,dinkwê		nnete
Time	lobaka; motlha; nakô	Try, to	leka, lekile
		Trying, to be	tshwenya
Tipsy	tagilwe; tlhapetswe	Tumour	boswa
		Tune, a	pina, dipina
		Turn aside, to	fapoga, fapogile
Tipsy, to make	tagisa, tlhapêla	Turn aside, to,to cause	faposa, fapositse
Tired	lapile	Turn round	retologa,
To (of infinitive)	go		retologile
Turn over	pitikolola,		

	phetsola		causative,
Turn, or go,	dikologa;		retolola
round as a	causative,	Vex, to	rumola;
wheel	dikolosa		tshwenya,
Turn, it is my	ke lobaka lwa		rumotsê,
	me		tshwentsê
Twice	gabedi		Village motsana,
Twist, to	sôka, sokile		metsana
Twisted	sokegile	Villain	molôtsana
Two	pedi, bedi	Visible, to be	bônala, bonetse
	with prefixes	Visit, to	lekola, lekotsê
		(the sick)	
		Visit, to	ja nala; êta
		Voice	lentswe, mantswe
		Vomit, to	tlhatsa; gôlôlêga
Udder	letsêlê; thele	Vulture	lenong, manong
Ugly	maswê; mpe		
Unable	reteletswe	Wade, to	gobua
Unbind, to	bofolola,	Wages	tuelô, maduô
	bofolotsê	Wagon	koloi, dikoloi
Uncover, to	bipolola,	Wait a bit	baya pelo; iketle
	bipolotsê		pele
		Wait for, to	leta, letile; êmêla
Under	tlase ga		nnêla, nnetse
Understand, to	tlhaloganya,	Wake up	tsoga, tsogile
	tlhalogantsê	Waken	tsosa, tsositse
Undo, to	dirolola, dirolotsê	Walk, to	sepela; tsamaya
Unfold, to	phutholola,	Walk about	tsamayatsamaya
	phutholotsê;	Walking-stick	thôbane;
	menolola,		seikôkôtlêlô
	menolotsê	Wall of stone	lorakô, dithakô
			marakô
Unkind, to be	tlhôka pelo	Wall of brick	lomôta; lebôtana
Unlock	kopolola;		dimôta;
	lotlolola		mabôtana
Untie	hunolola,	Wander, to	kgarakgatshêga,
	hunolotsê		kgarakgatshegile
Untwist	tshopholola		
Unripe	tala, sa le tala	Want, I want	ke a batla
Urine	motlhapô;	Wanting,	tlhôkafala
	morotô	to be	

68

Vaccinate, to	tlhaba, kenta	War	tlhabanô, ntwa
Vain, in	lefêla	Warm, it is	go bothithô
Valley	mokgatšha, mogôgôrô	Warm, to	omosa, omositse
		Warmth	bothithô
		Was, *see* It was	
Veil	lesirê	Wash, to,	tlhatswa,
Vein	losika lwa madi	(clothes)	tlhatswitse
Veld	naga	Wash for, to	tlhatswetsa
Venom	botlhoko; botlhôle	Wash	tlhapa, tlhapile
		Wash	tlhapisa,
Venomous, it is	e a bolaya	another, to	tlhapisitse
Verandah	mokatakô, maribêlô		
Very much	thata; bobe	Waste, to	senya, sentsê
Water	metsi (takes pronoun **a**)	Wind, the	phefô
Water, to pass	tlhapa, tlhapile; tlhapologa	Wind, to	sôka,,sokile
		Wing	lofuka, diphuka
Water, cold	metsi a a tsididi	Winter	mariga
Water, warm	metsi a a bothithô	Wire	mogala wa tshipi
Water, hot	metsi a a molelô	Wisdom	botlhale
Weak	bokoa	Wise, to be	go nna botlhale
Weaken, to	koafatsa	Wise,	tlhalefa,
Wean, to	kgwisa, kgwisitse	to become	tlhalefile
Weed	mofêrô, mefêrô	Wither, to	swaba, swabile
Weed, to	tlhagola, tlhagotsê	Witch, a	moloi wa mosadi
Weevil	tshupa	Witchcraft	boloi
Weigh, to	lekanya, lekantsê	With	le, or, na
Weight	bokete	With, by means of	ka
Well, it is	go siame	Witness	mosupi, basupi
Well, nicely	sentlê	Wizard	moloi wa monna
Well, a	sediba, didiba	Woman	mosadi, basadi
Were	ne or le, with pronouns;re ne re legônê, we were there	Wonder, to	gakgamala
		Wood,	dikgong
		Wood, a	sekgwa, dikgwa
Wet, to be	kolobile; metsi	Wool	boboa
What?	eng? -ng?	Word	lefoko, mafoko

What is it?	Ke eng?	Work	tirô, ditirô
When?	leng?	Work, to	dira, dirile
When	mogang, fa, e re	Worker	modiri
Where?	kae?	World	lefatshe
Which?	fe? with prefixes;	Worship, to	ôbama
	e.g., ofe, dife,	Worship God	ôbamêla
	bafe,etc.,motho		Modimo
	ofe? which	Worthy	tshwanetse
	person; selô	Wound, a	nthô, dinthô
	sefe? which thing?		
Whistle, to	letsa molodi	Wring-out, to	gamola, gamotsê
White	tshweu, sweu	Write, to	kwala, kwadile
Whitewash, to	taka	Write, to, to	kwalêla
Who?	mang? bomang?	Wrong	timetse, molato,
			phosô
Why?	ka ntlha yang?	Wrong,	dira molato; fosa
Wicked	bosula	to do	
Widow	motlhôlagadi	Wide	atlhame; bulegile
Width	boatlhamô	Yard	lolwapa, malwapa
Wife	mosadi, basadi	Year	ngwaga,
			dingwaga
Wild	tlhaga; mongala	Year, last	ngôgôla
Will	tla a; ke tla a ya,	Year, next	isagô
	I will go		
Year, this	monongwaga	Young	sa le nnye
Yearly	ka dingwaga	Youth, a	lekau; monana
	tsotlhe		
Yeast	sebedisô		
Yellows	tshêtlha, sêtlha		
Yes	ee		
Yesterday	maabane	Zebra	pitse e tilotsana

NUMBERS	DIPALO
One	nngwe fêla
Two	pedi, or, bedi
Three	tharo, or, raro
Four	nnê
Five	tlhano
Six	thataro, **or** rataro
Seven	supa
Eight	bofêra bobedi
Nine	bofêra bongwe
Ten	lesomê
A hundred	lekgolo
A great many	ntsintsi thata
More than a hundred	go feta lekgolo
A thousand	sekete
A million	sedikadike

SETSWANA - ENGLISH

VOCABULARY

Mo mafokong a a latêlang fa tlase fa, mafoko a e teng VERBS
(Madiri), mo Sekgoweng a rulaganngwa a laolwa ke **to**, jaaka mo
Setswaneng re dirisa **go**. Sekai:

> Akanya, **to** consider (ke go re, **go** akanya)
> Rata, **to** love (ke go re, **go** rata).

Lediri (Verb) le le supang tirafalô e e fetileng (Perfect), mo
Sekgoweng le etelediwa **have** kgotsa **has** pele. Jaana -

> Ke tsile, I **have** come; o tsile, you **have** come; o tsile, he/
> she **has**
> come; se tsile, it **has** come; re tsile, we **have** come; lo tsile,
> you
> **have** come; ba tsile, they **have** come; di tsile, they **have**
> come.

Lediri (Verb) le le supang se se santseng se tshwanetse go dirafala
(Future), mo Sekgowa e etelediwa **will** kgotsa **shall** pele. Jaana:

> Ke tla a tla, I will (or shall) come; o tla a tla, you will
> come; o tla a tla, he/she will come; re tla a tla, we will come;
> lo tla a tla, you will come; ba tla a tla, they will come.

A, let, a ba tlê, let them come

A, sign of a question: a ba tla a
  tla? will they come?

Aba, to give, to portion out

Abêla, to distribute to

Adima, to lend, or, to borrow

Aga, to build, to live, or dwell

Agisana, to make peace

Aka, to tell lies

Akabala, to be perplexed

Akanya, to consider; think

Akga, to swing anything

Akgêga, to swing about, to hang
  down

A ko, please (exigently)

Akofa, to make haste

Ala, to lay out, to spread out

Ammaaruri, truly, really

Amusa, to suckle

Anama, to spread, as branches

Anêga, to spread out to dry

Anya, to suck

Apaapa, to grope about; caress

Apara, to dress (oneself)

Apaya, to cook

Apêêla, to cook for

Apesa, to dress (another)

Apola, to undress

Araba, to answer

Ata, to increase

Atla, to kiss

Atlarêla, to take with both
  hands

Atlhama, to be wide

72

Ba, they, them
Ba, bile, again, also
Baakanya, to prepare, to get
　ready
Baa pelo, wait a bit
Baba, enemies
Baba, to itch
Baboga, to be scorched
Babola, to scorch, or, singe
Baeng, strangers
Baka, to praise
Bakêla, to cease from doing
　something
Bala, to count, to read
Bapa, to be side by side
Bapala, to acquire, to get by
　trading
Bapola, to peg out, as a skin,
　to crucify
Batla, to seek, look for, require
Batsadi, parents
Baya, to put, to place
Bedisa, to make to boil
Befêla, to slight (a person)
Bela, to boil, to ferment
Belaêla, to doubt, suspect
Belafala, to boast
Bêlêga, to bear, to carry, to
　have a child
Belesa, to cause to carry, to
　saddle
Belegolola, to unburden
Beola, to shave, to cut the
　hair
Besa, to roast, to bake
Beta, to choke
Betla, to do woodwork, to
　adze

Betsa, to beat, to punish
Betwa ke pelo, to be vexed
Bifela, to slight
Biloga, to spring up, as water
　in a fountain
Bina, to dance
Bipa, to cover
Bipolola, to uncover
Bitiêla, to patch
Bitsa, to call
Boagô, a dwelling place
Boammaaruri, truth
Boatla, stupidity, carelessness
Bobi, a spider's web
Bobodu, laziness, lazy
Bobowa, wool
Bobôkô, brains
Bobududu, greyness
Boboi, blunt, timid, cowardice
Bobola, to be ill
Boêla, to return to
Boemong jwa, instead of
Bôfa, to bind
Bofefo, light, quick
Bofêlô, the last
Bohibidu, redness
Bofofu, blindness
Bofolola, unbind
Bogadi, dowry
Bogale, anger, sharpness
Bogale, angry, sharp
Bogatsu, pins and needles,
　numbness
Bogisa, to oppress
Bogodu, theft
Bogola, to bark
Bogosi, a kingdom
Bogôbê, porridge

Bogôlê, deformity

Bogwêra, circumcision, ceremony

Bohula, greed, greedy

Bohutsana, sorrow, grief

Boifa, to fear, to be afraid of

Boijane, young locusts

Boikanyô, trust

Boikanngô, faithful

Boikhutsô, rest

Boikwatlhaô, repentance

Boitshwarêlô, forgiveness

Bokau, youth

Bokete, weight, heavy

Bôla, to rot

Boladu, matter, pus

Bolaya, to kill

Bolêla, to tell

Bolêlêla, to tell to

Boloi, witchcraft

Boloka, to save, to keep

Bolôkô, met dung (of cattle)

Bolola, to set out on a journey; cattle to go out of kraal, etc.

Bolotsa, to cause to go out

Bolôtsana, roguery

Bolwetse, sickness

Bôna, to see (pf. bonye)

Bonakô, quick

Bônala, to appear

Bonesa, to enlighten

Bonôlô, humility

Bontlê, beauty

Bontsho, blackness

Bonya, slow

Bopa, to form, to make

Bôpa, to bellow

Bopama, to become thin (in flesh), to starve

Bopelonomi, kindness

Bophirimatsatsi, sunset, West

Bora, a bow

Borethe, slippery

Bori, gentle

Boruma, soft

Bosa, bosele, dawn of day

Bosigo, night

Bosilo, foolish

Bosisi, harmless

Bosula, evil

Bosusu, deaf

Boswa, a tumour

Boswa, an inheritance

Bosweu, whiteness

Botala, greenness

Boteng, depth

Botha, to lie down (of cattle)

Bothologa, to set out, make a start

Botlha, sour

Botlhabatsatsi, sunrise, East

Botlhale, wisdom

Botlhe, all (of people)

Botlhoko, sick, sickness

Botoka, better

Botsa, to ask, enquire

Botsênwa, madness

Botsofe, old age

Botswêlê1ôpele, perseverance

Boupe, meal; flour

Boya, to return

Bua, to speak, to skin

Budula, to blow

Buisa, to speak to

Bula, to open

Busa, to rule, govern
Butswa, to ripen

Dia, to detain, to delay
Dibata, patches
Dibe, sins
Didimala, to be silent
Diêga, to delay, dawdle
Diga, to throw down
Dijô, food
Dika, to surround (as an enemy)
Dikanyetsa, to surround
Dikologa, to go round
Dikungô, berries
Dilola matlhô, to frown
Dimokana, to be giddy
Dintsi, flies
Dinotshê, honey
Dinyana, foolishness
Dira, war
Dira, to do, to work
Dirala, to become done, to come to pass
Dirêla, to work for, to serve
Disa, to herd, to take care of
Ditaya, to strike
Duba, to knead
Duêla, to pay
Duduetsa, to applaud
Dula, to sit down
Duma, to sound, to roar
Dumalana, to agree
Dumedisa, to greet
Dumêla, to believe or agree
Dupa, to smell, to scent
Dupêlêla, to follow scent
Dutla, to leak

E bong, namely
Ee, yes
E kete, probably
Ela, to flow
Êla tlhôkô, to obsere, to notice
Eletsa, to desire
Êma, to stand
Eme, standing
Êna, or, Ênê, he, she
Eng? What?
Êpa, to dig
Epolola, to dig out
E re ka, seeing that, since
E rile, when
Êta, to journey
Etsa, to imitate
Êtsaêtsêga, to be uncertain
Etswa, seeing that

Fa, if, when
Fa, at, by
Fa, go, give food to anyone
Faga, to put meal in to cook, or, make coffee or tea
Fa gare, in the middle
Faka, to flatter
Fala, to scrape with a knife, etc.
Falala, to be scattered
Falatsa, to scatter
Fale, yonder, over there
Falola, to escape
Fapa, to bind
Fapaana, to take turns, to pass each other; have conflict
Fapoga, to turn aside
Faposa, to make to turn aside

Farafara, to go all amongst
Fara, put on laps
Fata, to burrow, make a hole
Fatola, to split
Fêêla, to sweep
Fêfêra, to sift
Fêla, to come to an end
Fê1a, only, just
Felô, a place
Femêla, to defend
Fenosa, to make room
Fenya, to conquer
Fêpa, to entice
Fêra, to bend (a limb)
Ferikgong, January
Feroga sebete, feel sick
Feta, to pass by
Fêtlha, to bore, to make fire
Fetoga, to become changed
Fetola, to change
Fifala, to become dark
Fisa, to burn
Fitlha, to arrive
Fitlhêla, to find
Fitlha, to bury, to hide
Fitlhola, to have breakfast
Fodisa, to cure
Fofa, to fly
Foka, to blow (of the wind)
Fokotsa, to make less
Fô1a, to become healed, to
  recover
Fologa, come down
Foo, there, then
Fophola, to feel about
Fora, to hoax, deceive
Fosa, to miss

Ga, not
Ga, to draw water
Gaba, to scoop out
Gabedi, twice
Gadika, to roast,
Gadikêga, to have stomach
  ache
Gadima, to flash
  (of lightning)
Gadima, to look round
Gagaba, to crawl
Gagamatsa, to pull tight
Gago, your, yours
Gagogi, to become torn
Gagola, to tear
Gagwe, his, hers
Gaisa, to excel
Gakala, to be indignant
  (angry)
Gakatsa, to provoke
Gakologa, to become melted
Gakologêlwa, to remember
Gakolola, to remind
Gakolosa, to melt
Gakwa, ke, to forget
Gala, to scream
Galala, to grumble
Galê, always
Gama, to milk
Gamola, to wring out
Gana, to refuse
Ganêla, to dispute
Gantsi, often
Gangwe fêla, once only
Gapa, to take by force
Gapê, again
Gara, to coil

Gasa, to scatter
Gata, to tread
Gataka, to trample
Gatêlêla, to press hard
Gatisa, to print, to press
Gatoga, take foot off anything
Gatla, to strike (with a stick) etc.
Gaufi, near
Go, to (infinitive)
Goa, to shout out
Godimo, above, high
Godisa, to exalt, to cause to
    grow
Goetla, (or Gwetla) Autumn
Gôga, to draw, to pull, to smoke
    tobacco
Gokêla, to fasten
Gola, to grow
Golafetse, to be deformed
Golagana, to make an
    agreement
Golêga, to make fast, to inspan
Go le gonnye, a little
Golola, to unfasten, to
    outspan,
Gomotsa, to comfort
Gôna, gônê, there
Gongwe, perhaps, or somewhere
Gonne, because
Gopa, to rake up together
Gopola, to think
Gôra, to eat remains of food
Gore, that, so that
Gôrôga, to arrive
Gorometsa, to push out, to
pour out fast, or, make to
rush out
Gôtêla, to become hot

Hubidu, red
Hudua, to stir
Huduga, to remove (residence)
Huhula, to perspire
Hula,to graze, gather fruit
Hulara, to turn one's back
Huma, to get rich
Humanêga, to become poor
Hunêla, to tie (strings) together
Hunolola, to untie
Hupa, to drink a little
Hupêla, to be stifled
Hupetsa, to smother
Hutsa, to curse
Hutsafala, to be sorrowful
Hutshe, a hat

Idibala, to faint
Ikaêga, to lean on
Ikaêlêla, to intend
Ikana, to swear, or, take a vow
Ikanya, to trust
Iketla, to take it easy
Ikarabêla, to answer for oneself
Ikgapha, to be temperate
Ikgodisa, to stick oneself up
Ikisa, to take oneself
Ikhutsa, to rest
Ikôta mogatla, to wag the tail
Ikutlwa, to be sensible
Ikwatlhaya, to repent
Ila, to dislike, hate
Imêla, to burden to much
Imolola, to unburden
Ina, to dip, dip on
Ineela, to give oneself to
Inola, to take out of water
Ingôtla, to humble oneself

77

Ingwaya, to scratch oneself
Ipata, to make excuse
Ipaya, to pretend
Ipela, to be glad
Iphêtlha, to be unreasonable
Ipolaya, to kill oneself
Isa, to take, cause to go
Isagô, next year
Itatlha, to throw oneself away
Itatola, to deny (a fault)
Ithaya, to say to oneself
Ithiba, to restrain oneself
Ithuta, to learn
Itisa, to take care, take heed
Itôka, to complain
Itsa, to forbid
Itse, to know
Itshêka, to become clear, pure,
   clean
Itshekologa, to be impure,
   unclean
Itshêpa, to become pure, holy
Itshôka, to persevere
Itshôkêla, to endure
Itshophêlêla, to twine round
Itshuba, to hide oneself
Itshupa, to shew oneself
Itshwarêla, to forgive
Itsise, to give notice
Itsoketsa, to turn a ocrner, or,
   make a bend
Itsukula, to gargle
Itulêla, to do nothing,
   to be quiet
Itumêla, to rejoice
Itwela, to defend oneself

Ja, to eat
Jaaka, like, as
Jaana, now, thus
Jaanong, now, just now
Jala, to sow
Jale, lately, a while ago
Jalo, so, or, like that,
Ja nala, to visit
Jesa, to feed

Ka, with, by means of
Ka, can
Kaba, a fan, jackal's tail
Kaba, to plug, or, stop up
Kabêlô, a portion
Kabolola, to unstop, to ope
Kabola, to notch
Ka bomo, on purpose
Ka bonakô, quickly
Ka bonya, slowly
Kae? where? how much?
Kaêla, to instruct
Ka fa, according to
Ka ga, of, concerning, about
Ka galê, always
Kagô, a building
Ka gopê, not at all
Ka jeno, to-day, now
Kakanya, to tell, do declare
Kakê, a cobra (yellow) snake
Ka ke, cannot, ga a kake, he
   cannot
Kakô, lying, a lie
Kala, a branch, confidential
friend
Kalapa, to skip about
Kalo, so much, so great

Ka mosô, morning, tomorrow

Kana, to seal, to stop holes,etc.

Kaologa, to disappear, as mist, etc.

Kata, to tread

Kataka, to trample down

Katêla, to fill up a hole

Katisa, to break in, to train

Katoga, to move off from anything

Kaya, to describe

Ke, I, it is

Ke, by, with

Kê1êka, to examine

Keletso, desire

Kêmô, a standing, marriage ceremony

Kepu, a pickaxe's digging stick

Kêpô, a digging

Kgabisa, to adorn, to ornament

Kgabo, a flame, a monkey

Kgadi, honey beer, mead

Kgaka, a guinea fowl

Kgakala, far

Kgakgamatsô, a wonder

Kgala, to abuse, to revile

Kgaladua, a beetle (fruit-eating)

Kgalalêlô, glory

Kgalema, to scold

Kgama, a hartebeest

Kgamê1ô, a milking vessel

Kgampo, (or kampo) perhaps

Kganêla, to stop, to restrain

Kgang, strife

Kgantelê, presently, by and by

Kgantsadi, a man's sister, a woman's brother

Kgaoga, to be broken off

Kgaola, to cut off

Kgaoganya, to divide, to separate

Kgarametsa, to push along

Kgatha, to plough new ground

Kgatlha, to please

Kgatsha, kgatša to sprinkle

Kgêngwê, bitter melon

Kgêtha, to pay taxes

Kgetse, a bag, a sack

Kgoa, (kgofa) a tick

Kgogonoka, water-fowl, moorhen

Kgobati, bark rope

Kgobera, to stir up

Kgôkgôtshô, corner

Kgokong, a wildebeest

Kgola, to compel, to induce

Kgolaganô, a covenant

Kgôlê, a reim

Kgolo, great

Kgologolo, old

Kgolokwe a ball, a round thing

Kgomarêla, to stick to

Kgomo, an ox

Kgomotsô, comfort

Kgôna, to convince

Kgopama, to be crooked

Kgopisa, to offend

Kgora, to be satisfied

Kgori, a paauw, a bustard

Kgôrô, a gateway, a passage
Kgotla, chief's courtyard
Kgôtlhô, brass, copper
Kgotsa, either, or
Kgwa, to spit
Kgwanya, to knock
Kgwathisa, to beat, to punish one lying on the ground
Kgwedi, the moon, a month
Khai, cloth
Khiba, an apron
Khubama, to kneel
Khukhu, a beetle
Khurumêla, to cover
Khutla, to cease, to stop
Kika, a stamping block
Kilô, dislike
Kima, thick
Kinamêlô, a slope
Kitsisô, notice
Kitsô, knowledge
Koafala, to become weak
Kobô, a kaross
Koêla gongwe, to make a heap
Kokwaanya, to gather (things) together
Koloi, a wagon
Komakoma, to rain, a shower
Kopa, to beg
Kôpana le, to meet with
Kua, to shout out
Kua mosi, to send up smoke
Kubuga, wake out of sleep early
Kukunya, to bud
Kutlô, hearing, obedience
Kwaya, to lie in shade, to find something, as under a bush
Kwala, to write

Kwanyana, a lamb
Kwenne, thick, strong
Kwena, a crocodile
Kwatsi, a carbuncle

Laêla, to direct, cock a gun
Laila, to devour, (of fire)
Lala, to lie down, to lodge
Lalêla, to lie in wait for
Laola, to command
Lapa, to become tired
Lapisa, to make tired
Lapologa, to rest
Lata, to go to (a distant thing)
Latêla, to follow after
Latlha, to throw away
Latlhêga, to be lost
Latola, to deny, to announce a death
Latswa, to lick
Le, and, with
Leba, to look, to look at
Lebala, to forget
Lebêla, to watch, to guard
Leboga, to thank
Lebogo! not a bit of it
Lee, an egg
Leeba, a pigeon
Le fa, although
Lefa, to pay
Lefatshe, a country, the earth
Lefele, a rhebok
Lefifi, darkness
Lefika, a rock
Lefisa, to fine
Lefoko, a word
Legae, a home

Legala, a coal
Le galê, just so
Leganô, the inside of the mouth
Legapu, a water-melon
Legodu, a thief
Legou, a wild goose
Lehinini, Lerinini, a gum
Lehuha, jealousy, polygamy
Lehuma, poverty
Leinô, a tooth (mênô)
Leisô, a hearth, fireplace
Leka, to try
Lekakaba, a leaf
Lekape, husk, rind
Lekatane, melon
Lekau, a youth
Lekgwafo, a lung
Lekoto, a leg, a wheel
Lekotwana, a pillar
Lekuka, a milk sack
Lekwati, bark of a tree
Lela, to cry, to weep
Lelala, to look up
Lelata, a maid servant
Lêlêka, to drive away
Lema, to plow, or, pick
Lêmala, to form a habit
Lemena, a pitfall
Lemoga, to perceive
Leng? when?
Lengau, a cheetah, leopard
Lengôlê, a knee
Lenong, a vulture
Lentswe, a voice
Lentswê, a stone, a mountain
Lenyena, an earring
Lenyôra, thirst
Leofa, to sin

Leôtlana, an officer
Lepa, to watch carefully
Lepai, a cotton blanket
Lere, to bring
Leru, a cloud
Lesaka, a kraal
Lerama, or lesama, a cheek
Lesapô, a bone
Lesegô, a blessing
Lesilo, a fool
Lesogo, a partridge
Lesomê, ten
Lesomô, a party of people
Lesope, a ruin
Leswê dirty, nasty
Leta, to wait for
Lethatswane, a lapwing
Letlalô, a skin
Letlapa, a flat stone
Letlanya, to reconcile
Letlole, a box, a native corn
  bin
Letlôtla, a deserted house
Letsa, to play an instrument
Letsa molodi, to whistle, sing
  of bird
Letshoo, a paw
Letshwagô, a hole in a tree
Letsibogô, a ford, a shallow
  place in a river
Letsôgô, an arm
Letsomane, a flock of sheep, etc.
Letsopa, pot clay
Letswai, salt
Letswi, a grave
Letswele, a fist
Leuba, drought, farnine
Lewatle, the sea

Lo, you
Lôa, to bewitch
Lôba, to deny, to conceal
Lobaka, time, opportunity
Lobopô, creation, the universe
Lobônê, a lamp
Lodi, cord of bark, dinti
Loêtô, a journey
Lofafa, a feather
Lofarô, a cleft in a rock
Lofatsa, a splinter
Loga, to plait
Logadima, sheet lightning
Logong, a piece of wood
Logopo, a rib
Lohuba, consumption
Lohuka, a wing
Loisa, to thicken food (in cooking)
Loka, to season, with salt, etc.
Lolwapa, front yard of a house
Loma, to bite
Lomaô, a needle
Lomapô, a peg, a nail
Lomati, a board
Lomêga, to cup (medicinally)
Lomolola, to separate
Lomôta, an earth bank or wall
Lona, you
Lonaka, a horn
Lonala, a finger nail, or a toe nail
Lonyatsô, contempt
Looto, dim, dimness
Lootsa, to sharpen
Lôpa, to ask for
Lôra, dream
Loratô, love

Lore, dinthe, spear-handle, staff
Lorole, dust
Losa, to fight wild beasts
Losika, a vein, artery, sinew, a family
Loso, death
Lotlhaya, a jaw
Lotloa, a net
Loungô, fruit
Lwa, to quarrel, to fight
Lwala, to be sick, or ill

Maabane, yesterday
Maabanyane, evening
Maaka, lies
Maanô, plans
Mabêlê, corn, breasts
Mabôtê, bruises, soreness
Madi, blood, money
Madila, thick milk, curds
Mae, eggs
Mafoko, news
Mahumô, riches
Mahura, fat
Majê, stones, mountains
Mala, the bowels
Malôba, the other day
Mamarêla, to stick to
Manêga, to stick, or paste on
Manyêlô (mannyêlô), dross
Mang? who?
Maoto, legs, wheels
Maragô, hinder parts
Marang, rays of light
Maswê, nasty, filthy
Mathe, spittle
Matla, to canter
Matlhape, herds of cattle

Matlhô, eyes
Matsapa, labour, weariness
Mbu, soil, earth, ground
Medupe, a shower
Meênênê (Meeledi,), mirage
Mefêrô, weeds
Mena, to fold
Mênô, teeth
Metsa, to swallow
Metsi, water
Mina, to blow the nose
Minilosa, pour out last bit
Mma, mother, mme, my mother
Mmaba, an enemy
Mmala, colour
Mmele, body
Mmila, street
Mmoko, chaff
Mmusi, governor, ruler
Mmusô, government
Mmutla, a hare
Mo, in; him, her
Moagi, a builder
Moapei, a cook
Modimo, God
Modiredi, a servant, helper
Modiri, a worker
Modisa, a herd, shepherd
Modumedi, a Christian
Moemisi, a marriage officer
Moeng, a stranger, a visitor
Moeti, a traveller
Moetlo, anxiety
Moetlo, go jewa ke, to be anxious
Moêtsê, a mane

Mogakabe (Legakabe), white-necked crow
Mogatsa, husband or wife, spouse
Mogopolô, a thought
Mogotswana, a bowl
Mohama, side of a person, etc.
Mohana, a digging stick
Mofinyana, an axe, or, pick handle
Mofoka, tares
Mofufutsô, perspiration
Mohumagadi, a lady
Mohumi, a rich person
Moimana, pregnant
Moitlamô, a belt
Moitlhô, one eyed
Mojadi, a sower
Mokae? what countryman?
Mokala, a camel thorn
Mokatakô, a verandah
Mokete, merriment, party
Mokete, go dira, to make merry
Mokgôrô, a pole, the cross
Mokgosi, a loud shout
Mokhasi, rushes
Môkô, marrow
Mokoa, a heap
Mokole, a deep well
Mokong, a steep ascent
Mokôrô, a canoe
Mokôtla, the back, backbone
Mokwadi, a writer
Mokwaledi, a secretary
Molamu, a knobkerrie
Molaô, a law
Molaodi, a ruler, District Commissioner

Molapô, a valley, a river
Molelô, fire
Molêma, the left
Molemi, a ploughman, farmer
Molemô, goodness, good,
  medicine
Moleofi, a sinner
Molete, a deep hole, a dungeon
Molodi, a whistling
Moloi, a wizard, or witch
Molomo, a mouth
Molôra, ashes, soap
Mometsô, the throat
Monate, nice
Mong? What sex? boy or girl?
Mong, a neighbour
Mong, master, owner
Monna, a man
Mono, here, this neighbour-
  hood
Montlê, pretty (person)
Monwana, a finger, or toe
Monyadi, a bridegroom,
Monyadwi, a bride
Montsana, or, rnonang, a
  mosquito
Moôka, a white thorn mimosa
Mophatô, a regiment
Mopitlwê, March
Morafe, nation
Moragô, after, afterwards
Moranang, April
Morapêlô, a prayer
Morathô, a bridge
Morati, a lover
Morêna, Sir, a master
Moriri, hair
Morô, gravy, broth

Moroba, a young female
Morodi, rust
Morubisi, an owl
Moruti, a teacher
Moruti, or, moriti a shadow
Morwa, a son, a Southerner
Morwadi, a daughter
Morwalô, a burden
Mosadi, a woman
Mosese, a dress
Mosarwa, a Bushman
Mosetsana, a girl
Mošawa, river sand
Mosupi, a witness
Mosi, smoke
Mosidi, black powder, soot
Mosifa, a muscle
Mosima, a hole in the ground,
  a burrow
Mothêô, a foundation
Motho, a person
Mothusi, a helper
Motlha, a time, a season
Motlhanka, a servant
Motlhofo, light in weight
Motlhwa, white ants, termites
Motsana, a village
Motse, a town
Motshêganong, May
Motshegare, daylight, mid-day
Motshe wa badimo, a rainbow
Motsofe, an old person
Motswana, one of the Batswana
Motswe, a root
Motswi, an arrow
Moya, Mowa, a spirit, breath
Mpa, a belly, a switch
Mutlwa, a thorn

Na, to rain
Na, with
Naga, veld
Nakô, time
Nama, meat
Namagadi, female
Namane, a calf
Nametsa, to encourage
Nanoga, to rise up
Nare, a buffalo
Naya, to give
Ne ne, or, no no, should, should
   be, or, should have, *also,*
   would be
Nêêla, to give to, to lend
Nêô, a gift
Ngaka, a doctor
Ngala, to object to, angrily
Ngamola to stretch out
Ngapa, to scratch, to pinch
Ngaparêla, to stick to
Ngata, a bundle
Ngôba, to start after noon
Ngônka, to walk proudly
Ngôngôrêga, to grumble
Ngôtla, to diminish
Ngwaga, a year
Ngwana, a child
Ngwanaatsêlê, November
Ngwêga, to run away, escape
Nkga, to emit a smell
Nkgwana, a water pot
Nkô, a nose
Nkwê, a tiger, leopard
Nna, I, me
Nna, to be
Nnyaa, no
Nnye, little, small

Nôga, a snake
Noka, a river
Noko, a porcupine
Nôlô, soft
Nong, a large bird
Nôna, to become fat
Nonofa, to be able
Nontsha, to fatten
Nosa, to give drink
Nonyane, a bird
Nôtô, a hammer
Ntaya, to strike
Nthô, a sore
Ntlê, pretty, clean, nice
Ntlha, a point, an end, a side
Ntlo, come here
Ntlo, a house
Nša, a dog
Ntsha, to take out
Ntsho, black
Ntsi, a fly
Ntsi, many, plentiful
Ntsifala, to increase
Ntswi, an eagle
Nyala, to marry
Nyatsa, to despise
Nyôrilwe, thirsty

O, he, she, it, this
Ôba, to bend
Ôbama, to bend forward, to
   worship
Obola, to peel, to bark a tree,
Ogola, to take out of the fire
Oka, to betray, to nurse
Okama, to stand over, or above
Oketsa, to add to
Okola, to skim off

Okomêla, to look into, or, down
Ôla, to gather up, pick up
Ôlêla, to put into a sack, wagon
Ôma, to become dry
Ômanya, to scold
Omisa, to dry
Omosa, to make warm
Ônala, to get old (of things)
Ôpa, to slap
Ôpa, diatla, to clap hands
Ôra, to warm oneself
Osa, to cause to fall
Otla, to feed, to nourish
Ôtlha, to spin
Otlolola mabôgô, stretch out the
    hands

Paakanyô, a preparation
Pagama, to climb, to ride
Pagolola, to take down
Paka, to provide water for a
    journey
Padile, impossible
Palama, climb; ride
Palô, number
Papadi, trading, gains, goods
Papana, to make smooth
Papetla, flatten
Paraletse, stiff, astride
Pata, to accompany, path
Pataganya, to put side by side
Patêlêla, to compel
Pateletso, false accusation
Patika, to oppress
Patlê1ô, an open space
Pêba, a mouse
Pêga, to hang up
Pekanya, to mix

Pêlêgô, or Pelegi, childbirth
Pelesa, a pack ox
Pelo, the heart
Penologa, to overflow
Peo, seed
Pepetletsa, to drive carefully
Pelontlê, good-hearted
Pelompe, miserly, bad-hearted
Pelotelele, patient
Petlo, an adze
Pêtsana, a foal
Petsô, punishment, a beating
Phadimoga, to jump up suddenly
Phagê, a wild cat
Phala, a rooibuck or impala
Phalane, October
Phamola, to snatch
Phanya, to burst, to crack
Phanyegile, cracked
Phata, a poort, or, opening in
    Hills
Phatê, a skin for sleeping on,
    a carpet
Phatla, a forehead
Phatlalatsa, dismiss, disperse
Phatlha, an opening through
    trees, a gap
Phatsa, a chip, a splinter
Phatsima, to shine
Phatwe, August
Phekame, slanting
Pheko, a charm
Phela, to escape, to survive
Phelehu, a ram (sheep)
Phêmêlô, defence
Phenyo, victory
Phêpa, clear, innocent
Phêpafalô, dawn

Phepheng, a scorpion
Phetogô, a change
Phetsola, to turn over
Phimola, to wipe, to dust
Philô, a kidney
Phiri, a hyena
Phirima, to set, of the sun
Phitlhô, a burial, a funeral
Phohu, an eland
Phoka mahulô, to foam at the mouth
Phôkô, a goat ram
Phokojê, a silver jackal
Phôlôgôlô, a head of game
Photi, a duiker
Photha, to thresh
Phuduhudu, a stembuck
Phukwi, July
Phunya, to pierce
Phupu, a tomb, a grave
Phutha, to gather, to collect
Phutholola, to unfold, to explain.
Pina, tune, song
Pinô, a dance
Pitikolola, to turn a thing over
Pitla, to crush
Pitlagana, to be crowded
Pitsa, a pot
Pitse, a horse, a zebra
Pitsô, a call, a public meeting
Poane (Lwetse) September
Pobolô, sickness
Podi, a goat
Pogisô, persecution
Poifô, fear
Polaô, murder, a killing
Polêlô, a narrative, a story
Poloka, salvation (active)

Polokô, salvation (passive)
Poma, to cut off, to strike off
Pônô, sight
Pôô, a bull
Popêgô, a condition
Pôta, to go round a thing
Potlaka, to be in a hurry
Pôtlana, few
Potologa, to go round
Potsane, a kid
Potsô, a question
Pounama, a lip
Pududu, blue
Pula, rain; pula e a na, it rains
Puô, speech
Pusô, a reign, government
Potoka, (Putuka) to add together

Raêla, to tempt
Rafa, to take out, as meal, etc. from a sack
Raga, to kick
Raka, to arrive first
Ralala, to pass, or go through
Ranola, to speak plainly, translate
Rapalala, to lie across
Rapama, to recline
Rapêla, to pray
Rata, to love
Raya, to say to, refer to
Re, we, us
Re, to say, to do
Rebola, to permit
Reetsa, to listen
Rêka, to buy
Rekisa to sell
Rêma, to chop
Rêpa, to become loose

Repisa, to loosen
Rêra, to make a plot
Retela, to be too difficult
Retolola, to turn round (active)
Retologa, to turn round (intransitive)
Rôba, to break; to harvest
Rôbala, to sleep
Robegile, broken
Roga, to curse
Roka, to sew
Roma, to send
Rona, we, us; to be unbe-coming
Rota, to pass water (of animals)
Rôtha, to drop, of a liquid
Rra, rra, father, my father
Rua, to possess
Rudisa, to revive
Rumola, to, provoke
Rupisa, to circumcise
Rutla, to pull down
Rwala, to put on head, or feet, as hat or shoes; to carry on the head.

Sa, not, yet, still
Sa, bo a sa, to become light
Sala, to remain behind
Sama, to pillow
Sa ntse, still
Se, not, it
Seakô, an ear of corn
Seatla, a hand
Sêba, to whisper, to backbite
Sebata, a patch
Sebe, a sin
Sebedisô, yeast

Sebete, liver
Seboko, a maggot, a worm
Sebodu, decay
Seboni, a window
Sebopiwa, a creature
Sediba, a well
Sedidi, giddiness
Sedimonthole, December
Seditse, the brush at the end of a tail
Seêtêbosigo, June
Sefakô, hail
Sefala, a corn bin
Sefatlhêgô, face (of person)
Sega, to cut (with a knife)
Segô, lucky, a guard
Segokgo, a spider
Segolo, much, great
Segwana, a calabash
Sehohu, a blind person
Seipatô, an excuse
Sejô, food
Sêka, to go to law
Sekaka, a waterless country
Sekaô, a pattern, sample
Sekgono, the elbow
Sekgwa, a forest, a thicket
Sekisa, to try in court
Sêla, to pick up
Seledu, a chin
Selelô, crying, weeping
Selemô, summer
Selêpê, an axe
Selô, a thing
Semumu, dump
Senatla, hard worker
Senka, to seek
Senola, to make clear, or, to reveal

Sentlê, nicely, well
Sentlhaga, a bird's nest
Senya, to destroy
Senyêga, to perish
Seolo, an ant heap
Sepakô, a thing to carry water in
Serai, a trap
Serepudi, a step, or stair
Serope, a thigh
Seroto, a basket
Serwalô, a crown
Sesana, a stump of a tree
Seša, new, newly
Sesô, a boil
Sesupô, a sign
Sêta, to carve, to peel
Setlhabêlô, a sacrifice
Setlha, a bladder
Sêtlha, yellow
Setlhabi, a pain in the heart or chest, or side
Setlhake, an island
Sehudi, a wild duck
Setlhare, a tree
Setlôlô, ointment
Setou, fine flour
Setoto, a dead body
Setsênô, a mad person
Setshwantshô, a picture, a parable
Setswalô, a door, menses
Setswerere, neat, clever
Setilô, a chair
Sia, to outrun, to reserve
Siana, to run
Siame, to be right
Siamisa, to make right, or straight
Siamolola, to do wrong
Sibi, a piece of dry dung
Siêla, reserve for, pour out for
Sikara, to carry over the shoulder
Sila, to grind
Simologa, to begin
Simolola, to start something
Sita, to excel, to be better than
Sitwa, to be cold
Sôka, to twist
Sôkame, crooked
Sokolola, to turn (a thing) round, untwist
Solofêla, to hope
Sola, to smooth, to iron
Somê, ten
Sômêla, to push in
Somola, to pull out
Sotla, to deride, to mock
Suba, to hide (a thing)
Suga, to bray, to tan
Sulafala, to become bad
Sule, dead
Suma, to make a noise (like the wind)
Supa, seven
Supa, to shew
Supêla, to witness for
Supetsa, to shew to
Suta, to move away,
Swa, to die
Swaba, to wither
Swaila, to force a way
Swetsa, to finish
Ša, to be burning
Šapa, to swim, to beat

Šêba, to look round

Tabola, to dip out, with hand, spoon, etc.
Taetso, a message
Taga, to make drunk
Tagile, to be drunk
Tapeta, to bruise
Tatêla, to forbid
Tatlhêgô, loss, perdition
Tau, a lion
Tebêlêlô, expectation
Tebêlô, a watch, a guarding
Tebogô, thanks
Tedu, or, ditedu, a beard
Tekô, a trial
Tena, to be repugnant
Teng; deep here, there
Teseletso, permission
Têtêsêla, a trembling, palsy
Thaêlô, a temptation
Thaga, a sparrow
Thama, to be too large, to be happy
Thamô, a neck Thothi, a drop
Thoto, goods, possessions
Thuba, to break something
Thubega, broken
Thuga, to pound
Thula, to hammer, to do smith work
Thunya, to blossom
Thupa, a stick, a switch
Thusa, to help
Thusô, help
Thutlwa, a giraffe
Thutubulu, a rubbish heap
Tidimalô, silence
Tika, to aim at, throw

Tila, to avoid
Tima, to go out (fire), put out fire)
Timana, stingy
Timêla, to go astray
Tiralô, an event
Tisô, a herding, guarding
Tla, come
Tlaa, shall, will
Tladi, lightning (forked)
Tlala, hunger
Tlala, to become full
Tlalêlô, trouble, anxiety
Tlaletswe, anxious
Tlhôgô, the head
Tlama, to put on a girdle
Tlamêla, to provide for, to care for
Tletse, full
Tlhaba, to slaughter, to pierce
Tlhabana, to fight
Tlhabêga, to be startled
Tlhabisa ditlhong, to shame
Tlhatswa, to wash clothes, etc.
Tlhaêla, to fail, to come short
Tlhaga, wild, wary, grass
Tlhagisa, to warn, advise
Tlhagola, to weed
Tlhahuna, to chew
Tlhaka, a seed, a grain, a unit
Tlhakanya, to mix
Tlhako, a hoof
Tlhakolê, February
Tlhala, to forsake, to divorce
Tlhale, thread
Tlhalefa, to become wise
Tlhaloganya, to understand, to separate

Tlhaloganyetsa, to explain to
Tlhano, five
Tlhanola, to turn inside out
Tlhaola, to select, to separate
Tlhapa, to wash (hands, etc.);
  to pass water
Tlhapêlô, riot, noisy mirth
Tlhapolosa, to melt
Tlhase, a spark
Tlhatlaganya, to pile things on
  one another
Tlhatloga, to ascend, to go
  up
Tlhatse, below, beneath (tlase)
Tlhôafala, to be zealous
Tlhoba, to pluck
Tlhôbôga, to give up, despair
Tlhoga, to sprout (as a tree,
  or grass)
Tlhôgô e thata, stubborn
Tlhôka, to lack, to need
Tlhôkafala, to be scarce
Tlhôkô, observant careful
Tlhokofala, to become worse
Tlhôkômêla to take heed
Tlhokomologa to neglect
Tlhola, to remain a day, or
  a while
Tlhôla, to create
Tlhôlêgô, nature of a thing
Tlhôma, to plant, to compete
  in race
Tlhômamisa, to establish
Tlhômama, become firm
Tlhomeso, a rafter
Tlhomola, to pull up
Tlhong, a hedgehog
Tlhôpha, to clean corn, etc.

Tlhoro, a cap, a hat
Tlhôtlha, to strain liquids
Tlhotlheletsa, to incite
Tlhotlhomisa, follow up a spoor,
  to search out, to investigate
Tlhotlhorêga, to fall off, as
  leaves
Tlhwatlhwa, a price
Tlhotsa, to be lame
Tloga, to get up to depart
Tlogêla, to leave, to forsake
Tlola, to jump over, to trans-
  gress
Tlôla, to anoint oneself
Tlotla, to honour
Tlwaêla, to become accustomed
  to
Tokololô, a joint
Tomêga, to cup, or, bleed
Tonanyana, a male
Tôô, witchcraft
Tootso, a whetstone
Tôpô, a request
Tôrô, a dream
Tota, to increase
Tôta, self, itself, himself, etc.
Tsala, a friend
Tsala, to give birth
Tsalanô, friendship
Tsamaya, to go away
Tsaya, to take, to marry
Tse, these
Tsêbê, an ear
Tsela, a path, a road
Tsêna, to enter, to go in
Tsenya, to put in
Tshaba, to flee, to be afraid
Tshasa, to smear

Tshêga, to laugh
Tshêkô, a case in court
Thantholola, to unravel
Thapa, to hire for pay
Thapêlô, prayer
Thapô, a cord, a rope
Thari, a skin for carrying a child
Tharo, three
Thata, strong, hard, difficult
Thataro, six
Thaya, to make foundation; to set a trap
Thêbê, a shield
Thêkô, a buying, purchase
Thêla, to pour
Thêrô, a discussion, sermon
Thiba, to stop (a thing), to bock
Thiboga, to move out of the way
Thipa, a knife
Thitô, trunk, of a tree or shrub
Thôba, to break away, to run away
Thôbô, harvest
Thokgame, upright, correct
Thokô, aside on one side; an awl
Thopa, to plunder, take by force
Thota, a hill
Thotana, a rise, a mound of earth
Tshela, to live
Tshêla, to pour
Tshenyô, destruction
Tshepisa, or, itshepisa, to hallow
Tshiamô, righteousness

Tshimo, a garden
Tshipi, iron, metal
Tshipo, a spring have
Tsiang, a tsiang? What colour is it?
Tsiba, to cork, or to plug
Tsididi, cold
Tsiê, locusts
Tsietsa, to deceive
Tsietso, deceit
Tshikinya, to shake
Tshoga, to be surprised
Tshôkamô, crookedness
Tshola, to receive
Tsholetsa, to lift up
Tshologa, to be spilled
Tsholofêlô, hope
Tsholola, to spill
Tshôma, to speak a foreign language
Tshosa, to surprise, alarm
Tshôswane, an ant
Tšhôtlha, to chew up
Tshuba, to set on fire
Tshukudu, a rhinoceros
Tshumu, white faced (of animals)
Tshupa, weevil
Tshupêlô, an offering
Tshupô, evidence
Tshwaya, to brand, to mark
Tshwana, to be alike
Tshwanêlô, duty, right
Tshwanetse ought, worthy
Tshwantsha, to compare, to draw
Tshwanologa, to be unlike, to change

Tshwara, to take hold of, to arrest

Tšha, to dry up, as water

Tšhaba, a nation

Tšhaka, a sword, battle axe

Tshwene, a baboon

Tshwenya, to tease, vex

Tshwenêgô, vexation, trouble

Tsofala, to become old, to age (of people, etc.)

Tsoga, to get up, arise

Tsogêla, to get up early

Tsokotsa, to rinse out

Tsola, undress (lower garments)

Tsoma, to hunt

Tsônê, they (of things)

Tsopodia, round about

Tsosa, to make get up, to wake up

Tsuolola, to rebel

Tswa, to come out, (dule)

Tswaisa, to flavour

Tswala, to shut, to close

Tswêlêla, to go on, to continue

Tuêlô, a reward, pay

Tuka, to flame, to burn up

Tuma, to be famous

Tumêlô, faith, belief

Tumisa, to make a noise, make famous

Tumô, noise, fame

Tutuma, to roar, as flames

Twe, said; ga twe, it is said

Uba, to throb, to hit

Ubêla, to blow with bellows

Umaka, to mention

Ungwa, to fruit

Usa, to make to tall

Utlwa, to hear

Utlwala, to be audible

Utlwa botlhoko, to be sorry, to feel sad

Utlwêga, understandable

Utswa, to steal

Wa, to fall

Wêla, to fall into or, onto

Wêna, you, thou

Ya, to go

Yang, to what?

Yo, this (person)